P9-CAM-030

Meeting the Challenges of a Blended Family

Tying the Family Knot

by

Terri Clark

Tying the Family Knot
© 2018 by Terri Clark

Second Edition

Published by Timothy Publishing Services
Broken Arrow, Oklahoma

All rights reserved. No part of this book may be reproduced or transmitted in any form or by any means, electronic or mechanical, including photocopying and recording, or by an information storage and retrieval system, without permission in writing from the author.

Unless otherwise identified, Scripture references are taken from the NASB, New American Standard Bible, © the Lockman Foundation, 1960, 1962, 1963, 1968, 1971, 1972, 1973, 1975, 1977, 1985; used by permission.

Also included are: NKJV, New King James Version, copyright © 1979, 1980, 1982 by Thomas Nelson, Inc., Publishers; NIV, New International Version, © 1973, 1978, 1984, by International Bible Society; and KJV, King James Version.

ISBN-13: 978-1-940931-20-3
Library of Congress catalog card number: 2018940906
Printed in the United States of America

Text Design: Lisa Simpson

Contents

Acknowledgments

The whole Clark clan celebrates the publication of this book. Though my name is listed as having authored it, the entire family contributed to its completion. Without their support and encouragement, I never could have penned the first word. My deepest appreciation goes first to God and then to the many friends, family, and strangers who participated in this project by sharing their lives or lifting me up in their prayers. I love you all.

To Harvey, my beloved husband: thanks for your willingness to be transparent, reminding me of times, events, and situations to include in the chapters, for being a shoulder to cry on, for allowing me the time away to write, and for sending me roses. I love you.

To Jeremy, Jennifer, Aaron, Mandi, Sara, and Jodie: thanks for letting me make your life public. I pray God uses your lives to help others tie their family knot.

To Cynthia: thanks for praying for me, listening to my stories, taking the pressure off of me by handling paperwork, and just being my best friend.

To Monique and the Armor Bearers in Uganda, East Africa: thanks for praying for me. Nkwagala nyo.

Preface

How many of us as kids actually imagined ourselves growing up to be in a blended family? I know I didn't. It just didn't fit into my childhood dreams of marriage and family. Playing house with my friends, I never once pretended to be in a stepfamily. My perception of a stepmother and stepsisters was limited to the wicked old lady and two ugly daughters who mistreated poor Cinderella. I grew up on fairy tales and black and white TV programs where married couples stayed married. I never could have imagined any of my childhood heroes getting divorced and trading visitation rights.

My childhood dream was to marry Prince Charming, have a nice family and live happily ever after. Not unlike many Americans today, I found myself rudely awakened by life's realities and disappointments. At the age of thirty-five, I found myself divorced—a single mom with three children.

Prince Charming finally did come riding into my life on his less-than-noble steed. Harvey's old Chevy truck was more of a workhorse than a white horse, but then again, he broke all the fairy tale rules. My prince came with three young princesses and a castle in need of repair. With my daughter and two sons, I broke the fairy tale rules too. Jostling along with six children in our carriage, we had a long way to go down the road to happily ever after.

Your blended family story may differ a little from mine, but we're both traveling on the same road, hitting the same ruts and bumps of resentments, power struggles, exes, and visitation woes. To keep you from driving blindly, I've gone ahead to mark the bumps and ruts with road signs and directional maps to smooth out the ride.

Tying my own family knot proved to be a bigger challenge than either Harvey or I could have imagined. I looked for help wherever I could find it, but I only found articles and books written by psychologists or counselors. Most contained theories without solutions, stories without morals, and startling statistics without advice. Some questions were answered, but for the most part, I just wanted to sit down with a cup of coffee and talk with someone who had been there and done that. I wanted to ask them, "How did you, as a Christian, handle this?" "Did you get angry?" "Did you have a difficult ex?" The books and counselors were helpful, but I needed to connect with someone who had experienced the same emotions and pressures I was experiencing.

My prayer is that *Tying the Family Knot* will provide this connection for you. In it, you will discover workable answers for issues such as visitation, ex-spouses, court decisions, financial pressures, and stepsibling rivalry, while finding spiritual and biblical encouragement through hard, emotional struggles by someone who has been there.

As you travel down the road to happily ever after, you're bound to encounter well-meaning advisors along the way: those who will tell you it's not worth the trip, that you might as well turn around and go back the way you came. The world is full of easy outs, but in the end, those who choose to follow God, honor their vows, and remain solidly committed to each other will enjoy the scenery along the way. The road isn't easy, but with the light of God's Word to illumine the path, you'll reach that final destination.

Psalm 119:105 tells us that God's Word "is a lamp to [our] feet and a light to [our] path." In my years of blending, I found this to be not only a statement but a promise. Whenever I didn't know what to do about a difficult issue or how to respond to my stepchildren in love, God's Word would light the way. In these chapters, I've tried to share some of the wisdom and truth I found by the light of God's lamp, with the hope that it will light your way as well. So, grab a cup of coffee, settle back in a comfy chair, and let's talk.

Introduction

Like most moms, I have always had plenty of little sayings to get my point across to the kids. I pulled out my favorite whenever one of the kids couldn't find a lost item and I knew it was right where I told them to look. My phrase was, and still is, "Look like a woman." Why do I say this? Because a woman will lift things up and move things around until she finds what she is looking for. Most children (and yes, sometimes even men) will take a look on the surface, and if it doesn't jump out and bite them, they declare it isn't there. If you have ever lost anything of value, you can probably relate to a woman's sense of panic. I can.

On our first anniversary, Harvey planned an elegant dinner for us at the best restaurant in town. While we were on the way, he gave me some incredible perfume and lotion. Delighted with the gift, I opened the box to put some on. To prevent the lotion from getting into the setting of my wedding ring, I took it off and placed it in my lap. While we were laughing and talking and enjoying each other's company on the way to this restaurant, I forgot to put my ring back on my finger. We valet parked the car and went inside.

The next day I looked down at my finger and panicked. Where was my ring? I frantically tried to find it. Sick to my stomach over the loss, I searched the house and retraced every step I had taken over the last two days. After searching everywhere I could think of, it dawned on me—I was sitting in the car when I took off my ring to smooth on some of my new lotion. Immediately, I ran out to the car and combed every inch of it—unsuccessfully. With a lump in my throat, I prayed and hoped that it had been found at the restaurant.

When I called the restaurant, they told me one of the valets had indeed turned in a ring. It had been run over by a car and wedged into a crack in the pavement, but the sparkle had caught the valet's eye. Though the ring was bent up, he still saw that it had value. I was relieved and overjoyed at the wonderful news. I called all my friends to rejoice with me. My ring was found! The true value of my wedding ring could never be measured in dollars and cents. It wouldn't have mattered if my wedding band had been a paper cigar band; its value lay in what it meant to me.

Our blended family's value can't be measured monetarily either. We might seem a little rough around the edges at times, perhaps even a little tarnished. Divorce, remarriage, and the adjustments required to blend a new stepfamily have a way of dulling even the most brilliant gems. However flawed or tarnished, though, our family still has value. We need simply to step back and see them as God sees them—as hidden treasure, diamonds in the rough, ready to be mined.

In a blended family where we haven't had as much input into our children's lives as we might like, or when our kids aren't under our control, they might seem out of our reach. For a season, some may even fall away into the cracks of the world. But none of our children are ever out of God's sight. Their sparkle never escapes his notice. Our marriage, too, is a holy covenant. Every hair on our heads is numbered—however few. There are times, in the heat of an argument, when we feel defeated, as if we're losing our marriage. But it's not lost to us, just hidden. Because we are more precious to God than the sparrow, our marriage isn't lost to him either. If he can look after and care for the sparrow's needs, how much more will he care for his precious children?

Do you remember the story Jesus told of the woman who swept her house clean trying to find a lost coin (see Luke 15:8–9)? She swept and cleaned until her efforts finally were rewarded with a shiny silver coin. It didn't matter that she still had nine other silver coins. She knew the lost coin represented a day's wage. She worked hard for her money and wasn't about to give it up without a diligent effort to find it.

Did you notice in Jesus' parable that he used a *woman* as the one who swept and cleaned her house until she found the lost coin? He could just as easily have said a man or a child, but Jesus was born of a woman. He had probably watched his own mother sweep and clean their house.

As your family struggles with all the changes and emotions of blending your family, I want to encourage you to continue working and looking. Your treasure is hidden there somewhere—it's not lost to you. Don't just give a casual glance around the room either. You must "look like a woman"—sweeping under every attitude, moving past all the anger, and picking up all the emotions until God shows you the hiding place of your lost treasure.

In my panic to find my wedding ring, I didn't tear up my house, throwing everything around in my search. I did as the woman in the parable, who *carefully* swept and cleaned until she found her lost coin. I trusted and prayed that God would reveal the ring to me while I methodically turned over every inch of my home and car in my hunt. Faith and trust in God is the first step in finding anything that's lost—especially your family.

As you read through the chapters of this book, think of your family as a lost coin—a hidden treasure worth every effort to find. Don't give up the search because I'll be right here to help. Your diligent effort will be richly rewarded with the discovery of a wonderful family treasure and an heirloom of faith everyone can enjoy.

Chapter One

PUTTING IN THE SHOVEL AND DIGGING DEEP

Everyone who comes to Me and hears
My words and acts on them,
I will show you whom he is like:
he is like a man building a house,
who dug deep and laid a foundation on the rock.
~ Luke 6:47–48a

Before cellphones and text messaging came around, our teenagers had to use old-fashioned telephones plugged into the wall. Of course, that didn't keep them from talking all night to their friends. Our phone was really high-tech for the 90's, we had two lines—one for the normal family line and the second for the kids.

On that night, I could feel my jaw tightening and my blood pressure rising again. The red light on the children's phone line, indicating line two was in use, had been burning a hole into my calm resolve to keep my mouth shut. Ten minutes had passed since

I complained to Harvey that Mandi, his thirteen-year-old daughter, was on the phone twenty minutes past her bedtime. Harvey had responded by picking up the phone and, very gently, telling her it was time to get off the phone and go to bed.

Didn't he care that she was *still* on the phone? Wasn't he concerned that she was ignoring his "nice" request? Couldn't he see that she was being disobedient? It probably hadn't occurred to him that I was the one who had to go back to her room twenty times every morning to get her out of bed for school because she stayed up late on the phone every night. Harvey was lying in bed watching the news, oblivious to my rising anger. This was becoming a nightly ritual.

I had a choice. I could roll over and pretend to go to sleep, ignoring the red light on the phone; I could complain again to Harvey, knowing it would end up in another argument; or I could march into Mandi's room and physically take the phone away from her and play out the tantrum that was reeling inside of me.

The anger inside me didn't start building that night over the phone situation; it began when my stepdaughters came to live with us and the enforcement of rules became relaxed. We had very strict house rules before that time.

We gained custody of Harvey's three daughters a year into our marriage; they were ages eleven, nine, and eight when they came to live with us. My sixteen-year-old daughter and thirteen-year-old son were already living at home. My oldest son had graduated from high school the year we were married and had moved into his own apartment before the girls moved in.

On the surface the telephone problem stated above may seem pretty insignificant or trivial. In a normal biological family, it would be. However, in a blended family the discord runs much deeper; anger comes bubbling up to the surface by patterns of inconsistency and comparisons between children. Add a child's disrespect or disregard for a stepparent's authority, and you have the emotional equivalent of soda added to vinegar.

The pent-up anger I was experiencing is common in second and third marriages where stepchildren are involved. The U.S. Census Bureau reports that one out of every three Americans is now a stepparent, stepchild, stepsibling, or some other member of a stepfamily.[1] The National Institute of Child Health and Human Development (NICHHD) enlisted Dr. James Bray to study the stepfamily. One of the findings of his research was the high incidence of divorce in second marriages. He found 60 percent of these marriages failed, many within the first two years.[2]

Sadly, George Barna, author and founder of the Barna Research Group, finds that the divorce rate among born-again Christians and fundamentalist Christians is actually higher than the rate for non-Christians. Unfortunately, the Barna researchers discovered that for nine out of ten Christians who have been divorced, the split occurred after they accepted Christ as their Savior, not before.[3]

Every blended family is as unique and diverse as a fingerprint. Each one has different lines drawn from its own circumstances, personalities, past grievances, wounds, traditions, and habits. One family may be a combination of a widow with children and a divorcee, while another family may be a man in his first marriage to a divorcee with children. Some children live with the biological parent, visiting only on weekends; other children are already grown up and on their own. For some, the ex-husband or wife is easy to deal with; in other instances there is a constant battle. Some families come together with children who have special needs and handicaps; some have serious behavioral problems. The combinations are as limitless as the obstacles they must overcome. The big question is, how do we beat the odds and avoid becoming another sad statistic?

There is a lot of discussion about the blended *family*, but the bottom line is actually not in blending the whole family—it's in the marriage. Whether the kids blend or not, a divided marriage partnership reduces the whole family's potential for blending and staying together. The Bible says that a "house divided will not stand" (Matt. 12:25).

In my search for answers, I found three elements that must exist for a family actually to blend and for the marriage vows to remain unbroken by divorce.

1. *Christ* must be the foundation of the home.

2. Marriage partners must have a *commitment* to Christ and to their spouse with the understanding that divorce is not an option.

3. There must be an open line of consistent *communication* and *compromise* between spouses.

Any blended family combination can weave these three elements together into any given situation, and the family knot will remain tied until "death do they part."

Children grow up and set out on their own paths eventually. "Train up a child in the way he should go" (Prov. 22:6), is a charge given to us by God. If we recognize the authority of God's Word, allowing it to transform us into his image by doing what he says, we will see the vision of our own family knot being tied for life.

CHRIST AS THE FOUNDATION FOR THE HOME

It isn't enough simply to *believe* in Jesus. In Luke 6:46 Jesus says, "Why do you call Me, 'Lord, Lord,' and do not do what I say?" In the same way Jesus persuades us to act out his Word in our lives as Christians being conformed into his image; we are to live out our faith in our marriages and homes. Yet the hardest place to behave like a Christian is in our homes and around our family.

Jesus taught a parable in Luke 6:46–49, comparing two men building houses for themselves. The two houses were built on very different foundations. The first man worked hard because he wanted his house to last. It says he "dug deep and laid a foundation on the rock." Just imagine that guy digging and sweating for days, weeks, and months to get down to the solid rock where he could lay his foundation. Visualize his blisters and calluses. At the time Jesus told this parable, there were no backhoes around to make the job easier. The man had to have a vision of the house he intended to build as well as a determination to continue building. Jesus said when the flood rose and the torrent burst against that house, it could not be shaken because it had been well built. We all want to live in a well-built house that can withstand any storm.

The second man in Jesus' parable was not as diligent in his efforts. This man probably had a great vision of his house as well, but he didn't bother to do any digging. He built his house right on the undisturbed ground without any foundation. When the torrent burst against his house, it immediately collapsed into ruins.

The rock was there in both instances, and both men had a vision of the home each was building. Floods and torrents of wind hit both houses. The key to building a house that will remain standing after the storm passes is in the hard work of digging deep to lay a foundation upon the rock. In this parable, Jesus is very clear about the digging. He said everyone who comes to him, hears his words, and acts upon them can be compared to the man who dug deep. In order for our houses to withstand the storms, we have to be willing to work hard, get dirty, and endure a few blisters and calluses in our digging. We must dig not just until we *hit* rock, but until we've uncovered an area of rock big enough for a house to be built upon!

Acting upon the Word of God in our homes is hard labor. It is much easier physically to do the digging in a construction site than to apply the Word of God to our own emotions, especially when our children are at the center of the conflicts. We can call ourselves "Christian," but if we are not willing to do the work and lay a proper foundation on Christ the Rock, our vision of actually "blending" the family will end in ruin.

The act of digging deep is the daily application of God's Word to the hard emotional issues blended families face. Laboring—even when it hurts and you're worn down by repeated offenses—develops spiritual and emotional blisters. For example, when you feel excluded because your stepchildren reject your parental authority, it's time to put the shovel in the ground and dig into the Word. Keep on digging when your spouse seems to bypass or ignore your input on issues affecting the whole household. When you get down to Christ the Rock, lay your pain, anger, and frustration at his feet. He will give you wisdom, direction, and the ability to respond as a Christian. He loves you and cares more about you, your children, and your spouse than you do. He is able to work on your situation from the inside out. When you anchor yourself to that solid Rock, any storm can be weathered. The question is—How sweaty are you willing to get? How determined are you to see *your* vision for *your* family fulfilled?

In the telephone incident, I had allowed past grievances to build upon one another. My frustration was not just with my stepdaughter; it was focused on my husband even more because of his inconsistency in disciplining both sets of children. The responses I had allowed myself did not include surrendering my pride and anger. All three of the choices I had pondered had the same result—more anger. Life consists of daily decisions and continual choices because it is God's design for humanity. These choices are opportunities to anchor ourselves onto the Foundational Rock.

Because of my insistence on having things done my way, anger burned in me for two or three years. My way may have been right, but my unwillingness to compromise kept me from digging down to the Rock. Each small offense became another brick laid in contempt. I was like a pressure cooker ready to blow its top. It didn't take much to send me into a fit of anger; subsequently, I missed many of the small blessings of rearing my stepchildren.

During my angry years, I taught Bible studies in church and counseled other women in their marital problems. I applied the Scriptures to every other area of my life, thinking I was giving my *whole* life to the Lord. Outwardly, I was fine. My marriage was good in every other way. My husband and I agreed on most things, but the underlying emotions I felt every time we addressed a parenting issue were eating at the fabric of my marriage like poisonous and deadly venom. Nearly every day my husband and I found ourselves arguing about something the girls had done or had not done. These arguments were usually sparked by my own frustration.

Finally, in exasperation I cried out to the Lord for help. I read the parable of the two builders with the realization that *I* had been like the man who built his house on the ground with no foundation. I was not letting go of my pride or will long enough to break a sweat. Jesus arrested my attention when I read his rebuke: "Why do you call Me, 'Lord, Lord,' and do not do what I say?" My digging process had to begin right in my own backyard.

COMMITMENT

In our marriage vows we promise to love, honor, cherish, and remain faithful to our spouse—for better or worse, in sickness and in health, for richer or poorer, until death do us part. Yet divorce rates are soaring because houses are built without foundations and we renege on our commitment to each other. In fact, in a world where people change spouses as often as they change cars, *commitment* has become a foreign word. Obviously, this can be a touchy subject in a blended family. Unless both husband and wife were widowed, those in a blended family situation have probably experienced the tragedy of divorce. Separation by death is very traumatic; in most cases, feelings of love for the deceased spouse remain. With divorce, there is a kind of "emotional death" situation—while the spouse is still living.

Blending a family presents tremendous emotional challenges to any new marriage commitment, whether previously widowed or divorced. Walls and wounds especially accompany divorced couples entering a new marriage. These shadows from the past are difficult to overcome, but add children to the mix and you have the plans for a complicated house-building project. A solid commitment to Christ and to each other *must* be established! We need to recognize we are in this boat together. Our family knot will be tied securely only if Christ is the foundation for our home *and* we are committed to each other *until death do us part*. Divorce absolutely cannot be considered an option.

During one particularly aggravating confrontation, I was ready to walk out—walk out of the house and my marriage commitment. I left the house, slamming the door in confirmation of my resolve. It was around eight o'clock, and my mood was as dark as the night sky. In tears, I drove the twenty minutes into town. I got on the freeway, drove to the end of the freeway -construction, turned around, and drove to the other end of the freeway. I repeated this figure-eight on the freeway for three hours, allowing myself time to think, cry, reason, and pray. Finally, I pointed my minivan back in the direction of my home, concluding that no matter how upset I was, we were bound by a commitment and a covenant—made to each other in Christ—that only death would separate us.

Some of our family conflicts were extreme, while others were the "normal" blended family issues. However ordinary or bizarre your story might be, it is real and emotional to you, and you still have to walk through each situation with a commitment to Christ and to your spouse. Without this commitment, the vision of a completed house fades, and the family knot begins to unravel.

Once the marriage covenant is made, there is no looking back. Jesus said in Luke 9:62: "No one, after putting his hand to the plow and looking back, is fit for the kingdom of God." This may seem harsh in today's world, where quitting is an acceptable answer. Divorce *is* the easy way out. When questioned about the Mosaic law on divorce, Jesus said divorce was only permitted under the old Law because of the hardness of the heart (see Matt. 19:7–8). But Jesus came to change our hearts. When we commit ourselves to keeping our wedding vows, we have taken the first shovelful of dirt toward laying a solid foundation for our home.

Communication

Communication can be considered the nails that hold our house together. Through it we share our hearts with one another. More than just casual conversation, communication is a bridging of those hearts. Without it, emotions are suppressed inside of us like a smoldering volcano, eventually erupting with devastating results.

Christ, the Bridegroom, communicates with his bride, the church. His Word, the Bible, is an expression of his heart, communicating how he feels about every issue man faces. If we follow Christ's example of communication, we will share what is on our hearts in love, not anger.

My husband and I talked after my three-hour tour of the freeway. Our discussion continued into the wee hours of the morning, resulting in a method of dealing with all of our disciplinary problems. What I want you to see is how important it is to verbalize differences. After allowing myself to cool down, my husband and I were able to discuss the differences that led to my explosion. We were simply seeing the situation from different perspectives— each "right" from our individual vantage points. Compromise finally came through communication. Communication came by commitment, and commitment through faith in Christ.

Blending a family is an emotional undertaking. As twenty-first-century Americans, the world calls to us to demand our rights, telling us that if we aren't happy with the way we are treated by our spouse, just move on to someone else. That kind of living, however, only brings more pain and broken relationships into our lives. Not only are our lives affected, but our children can develop insecurities and psychological problems that will be carried into their own marriage relationships.

God has a better life designed for his children. As Christians, the Lord calls us to die to ourselves. This is a difficult challenge, but when we pick up our shovels and begin digging deep, the blisters eventually become calluses that protect us from the pain. The reward is a house that can't be shaken in any wind or flood. It will remain.

Chapter Two

New Faces at the Table

No one tears a patch from a new garment
and sews it on an old one.
If he does, he will have torn the new garment,
and the patch from the new will not match the old.
~ Luke 5:36 NIV

The wallpaper in the children's guest bathroom gave me nightmares. It looked like a big coloring book with partially colored characters of children playing happily all over the walls. The uncolored characters seemed to beckon any child who entered the room to pick up their crayons and finish the job. In fact, my husband obliged these happy little faces on the wall by giving his daughters crayons while they sat on the potty. Wisely, I held my tongue after seeing this wallpaper, but a notation was made in my mind to change it as soon as possible.

After Harvey and I married, my children and I moved into the house he had shared with his ex-wife and daughters. Because my husband's business is located on the adjoining property, moving to another house was not an option for us. I didn't mind living in this house, but the very thought of embellishing it with my own personal style of décor was energizing. Being a new bride, I was anxious to remove all traces of its former occupant.

As it turned out, complications in the property settlement from my husband's divorce prevented us from making any changes to the house. I had to live with those little faces on the bathroom walls for another two years. When we were finally free to make changes to the house, I was more than ready.

Approaching my husband with the idea of changing the wallpaper in the bathroom seemed simple enough, but I was unprepared for his response. He said, "The girls love that wallpaper, and besides, my ex-wife didn't pick it out, I did!" I don't know why it hadn't occurred to me before—only a daddy would choose that awful paper and then give his kids crayons to color on the walls! He explained that he wanted to encourage his daughters' creativity.

My argument was straightforward and had two points. First, the bathroom in question was a guest bathroom as well as the children's bathroom; I was worried about giving my guests nightmares. Second, if this was to be *my* house, I wanted to decorate it *my* way.

This debate continued for several weeks, usually on laundry day. The laundry room was at the rear of the bathroom in question. Those little faces sneered at me from the walls every time I walked through the bathroom to change a load of clothes. To my relief, Harvey finally relented, and the faces came down. The wallpapering was done while the girls were with their mother for summer visitation.

The new wallpaper was a simple design, matching the southwestern décor in the rest of the house. Harvey's house was finally becoming *my* home.

Everything was going well—until the girls came home on their weekend visit. They didn't seem to mind the main part of the house being decorated in my style, but when they went into *their* bathroom and there were no happy faces to greet them, attitudes changed. In their eyes, I had done more than just replace wallpaper; I had removed a vital connection to a past they were clinging to. The reality of their parents' divorce was still an open wound.

It wasn't really the little faces missing from the walls that posed a threat to the girls' world; it was the new faces at the dinner table. Although Harvey and I had been married for more than two years, the wallpaper change was a rude reminder of the fact that Dad was married to someone else. Adding sting to this tender wound was the realization that my children and I were living in *their* house, making changes while they were away.

Whenever two previously established families come together, everyone sees new faces. In fact, there were several new faces at our table. From Harvey's vantage point and mine, it was a marriage made in heaven. We actually thought our kids would be glad to see us happy.

Our children, however, were seeing these new faces at the dinner table not as guests but as replacements or intrusions. From Harvey's daughters' perspective, my three children and I were the new faces. From where my children sat, it was Harvey and his three daughters who were new.

Everyone at our table viewed the new faces differently from the old ones. The new faces didn't share the same memories, habits, mannerisms, or even looks as the old faces. For instance, when my daughter talked about gymnastics in the third grade, only her brothers and I could remember it. When Harvey's daughter told of their dog, Peewee, and his funny antics, my children and I couldn't visualize it because we had never seen him. Peewee was a part of the girls' lives long before my children and I entered their world.

My daughter and I love to make a silly "monkey face." My mother, brother, and several of my cousins in another state make the same face because our mouths are all shaped the same. Harvey's girls have tried to make this face, but they can't do it. Our physical bodies are completely different. Harvey's daughters are fairly tall, blond, and have fair complexions. My kids, on the other hand, are short and dark haired with olive complexions, like me.

Habits and disciplines were different as well. My children were used to a set bedtime and had regular chores. Harvey's daughters were permitted to stay up later if they were watching a video, and life was generally more laid back.

What did this mean? Would we never blend because we didn't share memories, looks, or habits? Of course not! However, in order for the old and new faces, regardless of perspective, to come together and actually become a family, a certain amount of stretching and shrinking had to occur.

My point is illustrated in another of Jesus' parables. Luke 5:36 reads:

> "No one tears a patch from a new garment and sews it on an old one. If he does, he will have torn the new garment, and the patch from the new will not match the old." (NIV)

I used to do a fair amount of sewing when my children were young. Because of my experience with cloth, I can easily relate to this parable. To patch an old pair of jeans with a new piece of denim, it is important to wash and dry the new fabric before sewing it into the old jeans. If I get lazy and skip this step, my work, no matter how skillful, pulls apart.

Expecting everyone in a newly formed household instantly to become a family is like sewing a patch of new denim into an old pair of jeans. Before an old pair of jeans can accept a patch of new cloth, this stiff, new fabric has to be "worn" a little and experience some shrinking and softening. In other words, a new piece of cloth must be properly "aged."

When the whole family moves in together—or even when part of it is separated, as in the case of another parent having custody of the children—everyone in the blended family has to make adjustments emotionally as well as physically. Each child needs to be affirmed and encouraged as to where *they* fit into this new family. Likewise, a new stepparent needs to allow time for everyone to adjust to these new faces, gradually and gently assuming a position of authority.

SHRINKING THE NEW PATCH OF CLOTH

In a blended family, the adults must do most of the shrinking. Why? The answer relates back to the topic of chapter 1: -digging deep—obeying God's Word in order to build our home on the Rock. Obedience to God's Word as a Christian adult is where the shrinking begins. Jesus said if we want to be first in the kingdom, we must be willing to be last. If we want our household to become a family, we moms and dads must be willing to make some sacrifices. Remember your vision of the completed house—that is your goal.

During our courtship my husband and I talked frequently about bringing our family together. We tried to be sensitive to what our children's needs might be, but nothing could have prepared us for the resentments and emotions that took root in their hearts. Most young children hold on to an unrealistic hope that somehow their parents will get back together and things will be like they used to be. Even in situations where fighting, abandonment, or abuse was the norm, children still love both of their parents. They usually remember only the good, or an imagined good.

Choosing Your Battles

Shrinking an actual piece of cloth requires putting it through a few washings. This takes time and patience. My husband and I learned through our own times of "washing" that it is best to choose your battles in order to win the war—or in our case, to see the vision of our house to completion.

Ideally, we wanted our home to be like a Christian version of *The Brady Bunch*. We drew the parameters, setting up "family" times, house rules, rewards, and punishments. We covered every base with every child. Our home was run like a well-oiled machine—until one of the kids was disobedient.

In a biological family, parents routinely discipline their children for minor offenses and then move on. Hopefully, the -children learn respect, and their character is developed in a positive way. The same minor offenses take on a whole new dimension in a blended family. While you naturally take into account the child's age, intent, and the normal "who started it?" questions, you also must consider how to handle stepsibling jealousy, attitudes injected by a bitter ex-spouse, resentments over having to "share" mom or dad with everyone else, as well as your own feelings of resentment or protection for your child versus the stepchild. This is where most stepfamilies fall apart.

Choosing your battles may require putting down the oilcan and allowing the perfect machine to squeak by with a few compromises. Why? Because our children are having to come to grips with a huge change in their lives. While bad behaviors that were permitted or overlooked before this "new face" came into their lives can change and be corrected over time, the real and immediate concerns that must be addressed are insecurities, fears, and resentments in the family relationships today. The way we approach minor offenses can make or break the family; therefore, they must be handled with compassion and godly wisdom. Evidence for Jesus' compassion for children lies in Matthew 18:5–6:

> "Whoever receives one such child in My name receives Me; but whoever causes one of these little ones who believe in me to stumble, it would be better for him to have a heavy millstone hung around his neck, and to be drowned in the depth of the sea."

Stumbling blocks come in many sizes and shapes. We stepparents can be stumbling blocks ourselves when we expect our stepchildren immediately to line up under our authority as a parent. I believe that it is in the context of humbling ourselves (Matt. 18:4) for the sake of children that Jesus said, "If your hand or your foot causes you to stumble, cut it off and throw it from you" (Matt. 18:8).

My husband and I had to "cut off our hands," so to speak, by letting go of our rigid rules in the minor offenses. Old habits are hard to break, "but as for a broken spirit who can bear it?" (Prov. 18:14). By constantly correcting and disciplining our kids over the things they had been permitted to do before, we diminished our effectiveness in the weightier matters. However, by overlooking the socks left in the backyard or a chore left unfinished, my husband and I could present a unified front in the really important family issues, resulting in effective discipline and counsel.

A STITCH IN TIME

Once the new patch of cloth has had time to shrink and soften a little, it is time to begin the sewing process. Sewing a patch over a hole is done one stitch at a time. It is a process.

God designed marriage so that a man and a woman would "become" one flesh. Having a ready-made family when we say our vows doesn't change God's design: it is expanded to include our children.

Differences and arguments over child rearing occur in every family—biological or blended. In a blended family, however, there is the one additional factor to take into consideration—"I've always done it this way."

One of the first arguments Harvey and I had was over how to fold towels. I was in the laundry room (with the sneering faces wallpaper) folding towels. My habit was to stand over the dryer and pull out one towel, fold it in half end to end, then over again, and finally trifolding it. After I folded the towel and set it on the washer, I reached for the next one and did it again until the job was done.

One day I noticed Harvey standing at the door watching me. I thought he was admiring his lovely new bride, who was working so hard to keep his home tidy. As I smiled at him, he responded with a comment on how I was folding the towels the wrong way. He said I should carry the towels to the bedroom and put them all on the bed to fold them. My adoring husband went on to explain that he thinks towels shouldn't be trifolded because they take up too much room in the closet. He demonstrated the "proper" folding method by folding a towel end to end, then in half again side to side, and then one more time end to end.

I retorted that the towels fit just fine in the closet, and -furthermore, I had been folding towels this way for twenty years— if he had a problem with it, he could do the laundry himself.

This exchange illustrates the fact that we all have our own preferred method of doing things. Both Harvey's way and mine resulted in clean, folded towels, but we differed on how to achieve that end. Likewise, we had each reared our children in our preferred methods. Neither method was all right or all wrong; both methods worked. But compromise was essential if we wanted unity. Both parties had to give something up in order to achieve harmony in our home. And as for the towels, we now roll them.

THE "CLOSED DOOR" RULE

Serious problems in the home result when parents air their differences in front of the children. It is important for parents to present a unified front in all areas of permission, discipline, and rewards. Children quickly learn to play one parent against the other if they sense that the parents are divided. Harvey and I managed to present a unified front on virtually every issue in our home. Early on, we agreed to take every discussion into our bedroom and hash it out behind our closed door until we came to an agreement. Seldom did we immediately agree on how to approach a situation. Sometimes our discussions became heated and went into the late hours of the night; but when we brought our decisions down to the children, we were in agreement. The children never saw or heard our discussions. As far as they were concerned, we were unified.

As an extension of our "closed door" rule, Harvey and I realized that our decisions were met with less resistance when the biological parent delivered the verdict to his or her own child. If it was a group issue, the word came from Dad because he is the head of the house.

This approach permitted each of us as stepparents to be accepted by the children. Resentments were avoided because it was a child's own mother or father who said no, or informed them they were grounded for a week. They couldn't point at the stepparent and say, "You're not my mother" or "You're not my father."

One stitch at a time, a new patch that has been softened through patient washings will cover the hole in a garment. As time progresses, so will your stitching progress. Before you know it, everyone in the family will be so comfortable with the soft, new patches that they won't even notice the repaired hole.

Chapter Three

TIES THAT BIND

Love never fails.
~ 1 Corinthians 13:8

So, what's your combination? My stepfamily is made up of Dad, Mom, my kids, and his kids. Do all of your children live with you? Are some grown and some still at home? Do you have children together along with yours or your spouse's children? Have you or your spouse been married more than once, with children from different marriages? In today's culture, believe it or not, living in some form of stepfamily is actually the norm for most kids. It's not uncommon to have several children living under the same roof with different last names.

What is a stepfamily? The *Oxford English Dictionary* defines *stepfamily* as a family with one or more stepchildren, a family in which at least one of the adult partners has children from a previous relationship or marriage, though not necessarily living in the same household. So if I understand this correctly, a stepfamily includes a mix of parents and kids from previous relationships in any number of combinations.

If mom and dad marry two and three times, bearing children along the way, their stepfamily tree could branch out in many directions. Some stepfamily trees have so many branches, they look more like bushes than trees. In fact, I don't think I have enough memory on my computer to hold all the different combinations of what might be considered a stepfamily.

Despite the variability, however, there exist common strands in stepfamilies that bind them together. Unlike nuclear families, which are tied by blood relation, stepfamilies are tied together by marriage and, most importantly, love.

I recently read an article in *Nightflying—The Entertainment Guide* written by Rosanne Cash,[1] daughter of the late Johnny Cash and stepdaughter of the late June Carter Cash. I say "stepdaughter" only for the sake of clarification because June Carter Cash banned the prefix "step" from their family's vocabulary when she married Johnny Cash in 1968. In a tribute to her "mother," Rosanne tells a story of how she was visiting June one day when the phone rang. June answered it, and for the next twenty minutes she was completely engrossed in her telephone conversation. After hanging up, June said, "I just had the nicest conversation," and she started telling Rosanne about this other woman's life, her children, where she lived, and on and on. Rosanne then asked her, "Well, June, who was it?" to which June promptly replied, "Why, honey, it was a wrong number."[2]

Rosanne explains, "That was June. In her eyes there were two kinds of people in the world: those she knew and loved, and those she didn't know and love. She looked for the best in everyone; it was a way of life for her."[3] The moment people entered June's world, they were no longer strangers.

If we could take this a "step" further, especially as Christians in a blended family, the moment our stepchildren enter our world, they are no longer "his" or "her" children; rather, they are "our" children—children we are getting to know and whom we choose to love.

Rosanne Cash's tribute to her stepmother is an example of love's binding tie. June didn't give Rosanne or her other two sisters birth, but June still viewed them as her children—the same as her own two daughters and the son she and Johnny had together. They were a family tied together by marriage and love.

If we would remove our "step" blinders for a moment, we would see that June was living out Jesus' instructions to love as we want to be loved. If, however, we choose to keep our "step" blinders over our eyes by mentally drawing a division between "yours," "mine," and "ours," our family will always be a "stepfamily," and tying an enduring family knot will be very difficult.

The whole idea of marriage is a lifetime commitment. When we vow to love our spouse, it's a package deal—until death do us part. "His" and "her" children become "our" children. In the beginning, love is a choice. After we've had time to blend, love becomes a natural part of the relationship between parent and child. Sure, by *Oxford*'s definition anyone else would call us a stepfamily. That's OK, but as far as we, the parents, are concerned, we're a family without barriers—however newly formed we might be.

What Do I Call Him?

Entering into a marriage with children poses all kinds of unique situations. One is determining how the new stepparent should be addressed by the child. Should we insist they call us Mom or Dad? Is it proper for a child to address an adult by his or her first name? This is one of the first questions to surface after individuals with children marry.

I noticed in Rosanne Cash's article that she addressed her stepmother as "June" in their conversation about the lady who called the wrong number. She said, "Well, June, who was it?" You could tell by the article that Rosanne had a deep admiration and love for June, so she wasn't being disrespectful in addressing her stepmother by her given name. Neither did June's response hold any animosity toward Rosanne for using her first name because she affectionately addressed her as "honey." If June banned the prefix "step" from their family's vocabulary, why wouldn't she expect Rosanne to address her as Mom?

My stepdaughters call me Terri, and my children call Harvey by his given name as well. We've never insisted any of our stepchildren call us Mom or Dad. You might ask us the same question. If we've removed our "step" blinders and all the barriers separating stepparent and child, why wouldn't we insist on being called Mom or Dad?

I'm glad you asked. June, Harvey, and I all entered our marriages embracing our stepchildren as our own. That doesn't mean, however, our children embraced us as their parents. Acceptance took time. That is what blending is all about. In the beginning, acceptance is very one-sided. My stepdaughters already had a mother. She was Mom. I was their dad's new wife, Terri. The same is true for my children and Harvey.

Over time, as the family begins to blend together, the children grow to accept their stepparent as a permanent part of their lives. We can't force acceptance or love. This comes through interaction and consistently loving our children. To insist that our new children call us Mom or Dad would be to insist that they betray their natural mom or dad. This isn't a good way to start blending a family. But if you, as a parent, have removed the mental barriers of "yours," "mine," and "ours," your stepchildren will eventually remove them as well. Even though they may still call you by your first name, they will think of you as mom or dad.

My kids love Harvey. He has become their dad over the years because he was there for them when they needed help, he corrected them in love, and he supported them in their life endeavors. Harvey has laughed and had fun with my kids the same as with his own. Jeremy, Jennifer, and Aaron all introduce Harvey to other people by saying, "This is my dad." They aren't betraying their natural father in doing this, but they're acknowledging Harvey as another parent, bound by love. For all practical purposes, Harvey is their dad, but they still address him as Harvey—and that's just fine with him.

In instances where the child is very young and has no relationship with their natural parent, the stepparent will become mom or dad to that child much sooner and will subsequently wear the title Mom or Dad much sooner. This was the case with my friend who was widowed with five children. The two youngest children were three and eighteen months at the time of their father's death. Both call their new stepfather Daddy, while the three older children, who remember their father very well, call their stepfather by his first name. Too young to remember their natural father, the youngest children will probably always think of their stepdad as Daddy. In time, the older children will probably grow to think of their stepfather as dad, too, but they'll probably never address him as Daddy, as do their younger siblings.

If your children do not live with you because of custody arrangements, blending into your new family will naturally prove more difficult and take longer. The child living elsewhere may never think of your spouse as mom or dad. This is only natural. You should keep in mind that it is not the child's responsibility to remove those "step" barriers; it is for the parent to remove them. When your son or daughter comes to visit, they should be included as part of your family, regardless of whether they live in your house full- or part-time. Feelings of rejection come easily to a child who is treated differently.

Sometimes the child makes it difficult for the parents to embrace him or her, especially in adolescence. Several things can color their view of your family. One reason for their rejection or resentment can come from bad feelings injected by the natural parent. Their view can also be tainted by pent-up anger over the divorce, jealousies of other children in the home, or mistrust of the remarriage. Yet parents must be careful in their evaluations of a child's behavior. An adolescent's busy life with his or her friends may be misinterpreted as a rejection when it is not.

Regardless of the reason behind your child's rejection of you and your spouse, you both should make every effort to embrace him as a part of your family. Love is a choice. Don't stop reaching out to your teen who doesn't live with you just because he doesn't take the initiative to call or visit. If nothing else, your attempt to talk to him on the phone lets him know that you love him and that he is still important to you. In later years he will remember your love and know the door is always open for him to have a relationship with you. If you give up and quit calling because he never seems to have time for you, the door may never open.

The funny and reassuring thing about adolescence is that it passes. An adolescent eventually does grow up and move past his self-centered ways. My kids, in particular my stepdaughters, have come back to me in their young adulthood and apologized for being so difficult as teens. The oldest even asked me, while observing her younger sibling's obnoxious behavior, "Was I like that?" When I answered, "Worse," she replied, "I'm really sorry, Terri." The Bible says in Romans 12:18: "So far as it depends on you, be at peace with all men." This includes difficult children. If we, as parents, hold fast to our choice to love difficult children, eventually, they will accept us, even if it is just a cordial acceptance.

LOOSE ENDS

Finding acceptance from within the family can prove difficult enough, but gaining acceptance and understanding from outside the immediate family can introduce another realm of challenges. Grandparents, aunts, uncles, and even old family friends who have known you all your life and have had a relationship with you and your ex-spouse might have trouble welcoming your new family. Even if they completely understand the reasons for the divorce, just the fact that they don't really know your new husband and his children is enough to keep them from embracing this new set of relatives.

Outwardly, they might accept them, but if they live in another town without the opportunity to get close to your new family members, they will find it hard to think of the whole family as a new unit. For example, your parents may have eagerly waited for news of your children's births. They send the children Christmas cards and gifts on birthdays. A holiday never passes that they don't send a special card to their wonderful grandkids. Grandma even carries pictures of her grandchildren in her wallet, showing them off to everyone, even strangers standing in line at the post office. Got the picture?

In the meantime, you've been through a very difficult divorce or the death of your spouse. Time has passed, and Grandma and Grandpa still send cards and gifts. Along comes a wonderful new person into your life, and you remarry. He has a six-year-old daughter named Susie. At the wedding, Grandma and Grandpa welcome the new man and his daughter into the family. You tell them little Susie's birthday, but when the day comes, they forget it. A month later your own child has a birthday and gets showered with gifts, money, and phone calls from Grandma and Grandpa.

Grandparents are only human. The oversight wasn't intentional. Their new stepgrandaughter's birthday isn't a date they are used to celebrating. They weren't there when she was born, and they may have only been around her a few times. However, this is the kind of loose end one might expect to encounter while tying a family knot. You and your spouse may think of yourselves with all the children as a family, but that idea hasn't set itself into the minds of your extended family yet.

Go easy on your family and friends. Help them out by reminding them early that an important birthday is coming up. If they forget, or don't accept your new family, do what you can to protect the children from being hurt by talking to them. Not everyone is going to have the perfect family with total acceptance. The important thing is that you and your spouse don't allow extended family and friends to keep you from making your children feel special.

You can also help your extended family to accept your new family by talking about the new members. When you receive a phone call asking about the kids, the caller may be referring to "your" kids, but go ahead and fill them in on what *everyone* in the family is doing. This sends the message that you think of everyone as part of your family, not just the "original" ones. In time, extended family members will also include everyone in their thinking. Harvey and I have been married thirteen years, and our extended families still don't always include everyone in their thinking. But then, I don't always remember everyone's birthday either. We're all humans, saved by grace.

Everyone slips up and is in need of forgiveness from time to time. Jesus stressed the importance of forgiving others for their transgressions in Matthew 6:14–15 when he said, "For if you forgive others for their transgressions, your heavenly Father will also forgive you. But if you do not forgive others, then your Father will not forgive your transgressions." Now that's a convicting thought! Our extended family and friends may say or do things that hurt our feelings or the feelings of someone in our family; but these types of rejections, whether intentional or not, must be forgiven. We've been forgiven much more by God.

With grandparents in mind, I want to bring up another loose end. While we want our new spouse's parents to be included in our family lives, we don't want to cut all ties to the children's natural grandparents. Yes, you may have divorced their son or daughter, but your children are still their flesh and blood grandchildren. They were there when the children were born, and they do have an attachment. Not only do they have an attachment to the children, but the children have an attachment to them. They love their grandma and grandpa and shouldn't be deprived of this relationship. If a grandparent wants to talk to the children on the phone, or if they want to take them out for an evening, you should promote this relationship instead of hindering it.

There are those situations where the grandparents haven't been in the children's lives or where tension—even hatred—exists. If that is the case, I advise letting the grandparents arrange time with the children solely through your ex-spouse. The main thing is to remember Romans 12:18: "If possible, so far as it depends on you, be at peace with all men."

LOOSE TIES

Loose ties are the relationships developed during a couple's marriage that remain tied after a divorce or death. Sometimes these are close friendships developed between the husband or wife and their former brother-, sister-, uncle-, aunt-, mother- or father-in-law. These relationships can remain intact for a lifetime.

A biblical example is Ruth and Naomi. Blood didn't tie them together—it was marriage and love. Naomi was Ruth's mother-in-law, but their tie wasn't cut when Ruth's husband died. Ruth wouldn't allow anything but death to separate them. Many step connections have that same bond.

Your new spouse may find it difficult to understand why you want to have anything to do with your ex's family. He or she may try to make friendships with former in-laws difficult to maintain after remarriage. As with all the other issues in your new marriage, communication is the key. Talk and pray about this together. If you can carry on the friendship without driving wedges in your new marriage, keep talking. But if the friendship is a constant source of contention, lay it down. "If your hand or your foot causes you to stumble, cut it off and throw it from you" (Matt. 18:8). In other words, if this relationship causes your marriage to splinter, perhaps it is time to cut the old strings.

Not all bonds are between the couple and former in-laws. Some include relationships between the children and their stepparent. That stepparent and child can grow very close, especially if the stepparent has been a child's only dad or mom -during the more impressionable years of growing up.

I know of a young woman whose mother divorced her dad when she was two. A short time later her mother remarried. Because the child didn't have much contact with her biological father, the stepfather became like a dad to her. When she was nine years old, however, her stepfather and mother divorced. As far as this young girl was concerned, her stepfather will always be her dad. He was there for her in her formative years and continues to be a part of her life, even though he and her mother have been divorced for many years. There is no blood relationship, but there is a tie binding them—love.

The young woman told me that many people don't understand that they *are* father and daughter. Occasionally people outside of this relationship have asked the stepfather why he stays in touch with his "former" stepdaughter. "After all," they say, "she's not your 'real' daughter." To this he replies, "Well, she's not a 'fake' daughter." The fact that the mother and former stepfather aren't married anymore doesn't mean that the father-daughter relationship has to end as well.

Relationships like the above are more common than you might think, and stepfamily structures can become quite complex. Sadly, divorce has created a whole new definition of what *family* means to many of us. Blending a family is more than a husband and wife marrying with children; it includes a whole gamut of family ties. I still have great respect and affection for my former in-laws, and my husband still has ties to some of his. Our children have connections to relatives on both sides of our families and on both sides of our exes' family. Some they know well; some they've barely met.

If you want to know just how complex your stepfamily is, try and make up a family tree for one of your kids. Our family *bush* now has branches running everywhere. I can only imagine what a mess it will be in a hundred years for our poor ancestors attempting to piece together a family genealogy.

Regardless of where you or your spouse's family ties connect and disconnect, we all must keep our purpose in front of us— tying our family into an enduring knot. The first thing we do is to remove the mental "step" barriers by following June Carter Cash's example and banning—at least mentally—the prefix "step" from our home.

Forgiving past wrongs is critical to an enduring knot. The storm of divorce can leave devastation in its wake. Like lightning striking a family tree, divorce splits the most important relationship in our children's young lives—their parents' relationship. This is a tremendous loss in itself, but permitting the winds of unforgiveness to blow through your home will cause an even deeper loss for your children. Cutting off contact with their grandparents or a favorite uncle might make your life less complicated, but what about your children's? Maintaining healthy relationships with people important to our children speaks volumes in the language of love.

A solid marriage and family can mean the beginning of healing for our children. Loose ends are always found blowing in the winds of divorce. Love and forgiveness are a choice. A little rustling in the branches of the family bush might chase out a few unwanted birds, but if we want our family to remain a family, we need to hold it together with love and forgiveness—the ties that bind.

Chapter Four

Tying the Family Knot

These stones shall become a memorial. . . .
~ Joshua 4:7

Every Christmas I say I'm not going to hang up the reindeer, and every year I'm met with protests and gasps of disbelief. I made the big stuffed Rudolph head, with a wreath hanging around his neck, out of Christmas calico fabrics the first year Harvey and I were married. Rudolph's traditional spot is above the fireplace mantle overlooking the many stockings waiting to be filled on Christmas Eve. That first year I wanted the holiday to be festive and fun for all the kids, so I made the reindeer and matching stockings for everyone in the family. Over the years the number of stockings has multiplied, and Rudolph has become a little limp, but it just wouldn't seem like Christmas without them. The reindeer and stockings are as much a part of our family's Christmas as the tree.

When I was sewing these Yuletide decorations, I had no idea they would become an important part of our family tradition. Every year we seem to add a new stocking because of a marriage or birth in the family. We are now up to seventeen stockings hanging across the mantle under Rudolph's watchful eye. There seems to be something special about seeing the whole family together across the mantle. When friends and visitors come into the house, they cannot deny the sense of "family."

When our grandchildren come to visit at Christmastime, they walk past all my carefully placed holiday decorations in the rest of the house and head straight to the reindeer and stockings. Checking to see if the stocking bearing his or her name is hanging in its place, the children often ask, "Grandma, why do you have so many stockings hanging up?" or "What are you going to do when you run out of room?"

Their questions remind me of the children of Israel crossing over the Jordan River into the Promised Land. Once the entire nation—with all their animals and possessions—crossed to the other side, God told Joshua to take up twelve stones from the middle of the Jordan, carry them to the other side, and stand them up. In anticipation of the obvious question "Why?" Joshua explained:

> "When your children ask later, saying, 'What do these stones mean to you?' then you shall say to them, 'Because the waters of the Jordan were cut off before the ark of the covenant of the Lord; when it [the ark] crossed the Jordan, the waters of the Jordan were cut off.' *So these stones shall become a memorial to the sons of Israel forever.*" (Josh. 4:6–7, italics added)

Our Christmas stockings are a memorial to our sons and daughters as well. When my grandchildren ask me why I have so many stockings hanging up, I tell them it is because everyone in the family is special and important, and I could never leave anyone out. There will always be room for everyone, even if I have to scrunch all the stockings on top of one another. The reindeer and all of the stockings are a memorial to what God has done to make every name on every stocking a part of our family.

Joshua didn't pass through the waters alone. The individual stones represented each one of the twelve tribes of Israel; but together, the twelve stones were a memorial and a symbol of what a sovereign God can do with a nation that follows him in unity. The journey had been no easy feat for Joshua or the bickering tribes. Likewise, achieving unity as a blended family is a challenge that becomes a reality one step at a time. What seemed to me at times to be an impossible trek has become a testimony of God's grace. When we set our faces to follow him, he parts the waters for us.

Allowing God to lead is especially important in a blended family because of the unique challenges we face. One of those challenges is achieving the sense of *being* a family. When everyone comes together in the beginning, no one really feels like they are part of a "family." In fact, the children may feel somewhat threatened by the sudden changes and the prospect of getting "lost in the sauce."

I have been curious for years about who came up with the term *blended family*. Being a mom who cooks, I think the term *blend* suggests combining all of the ingredients until they lose their individual identity, becoming a smooth sauce without lumps. Nothing could be further from reality when it comes to "blending" a family. In fact, I would describe our ready-made families as "sautéed" because each ingredient has its own distinct characteristics. All of the ingredients are tossed together into one pan and cooked quickly over high heat. Each ingredient complements the others while maintaining its own identity. This process creates a delicious combination of flavor and texture. We want our family to come together, while maintaining every member's personality and style.

Actually, a sense of family and tradition is achieved when every part of the body comes together and functions as a whole. The things we do together become the times, memories, events, and customs unique to our family. These remembrances and traditions are our legacy and our children's inheritance. They become the cords that bind us together.

TYING THE FRAYED ENDS TOGETHER

Because the cords of a blended family are frayed when they first come together, we must be careful not to tangle the ends in the process of tying our knot. The best way to do this is by starting fresh—creating and building brand-new traditions and memories.

When Harvey and I married, I became a shutterbug because neither one of us had many pictures of our kids. Having pictures taken by a professional photographer was expensive and a lot of trouble, but snapping photos was fun, easy, and cheap. I kept my camera loaded and within easy reach all the time. My family will testify that I was always snapping candid photos of everyone, nearly every day. A fresh roll of film was loaded into the camera as quickly as the last one was finished. I took so many pictures that the film developer and I were on a first-name basis. As soon as I brought the pictures home, they went straight into the photo album where the kids would sprawl out on the floor and talk about Mandi's great cheerleading jump on the trampoline or the pouty face Jodie made when she didn't get her way. Birthday parties were relived and special moments recounted. Our first photo album is so worn from years of looking at it that the binding has completely separated from the three rings that hold the pages together. At last count I think we had twenty filled photo albums.

"Capturing the moment" has become a Clark family tradition. Recording both the fun moments in our daily lives as well as the special events on film accidentally caused everyone in our house to come together as a family. I say "accidentally" because my original intent in taking the pictures was simply to *have* pictures. I never anticipated the albums bringing such unity between the kids.

Of course, just taking pictures at home isn't enough to actually make a blended family come together. Orchestrating special events and fun times to photograph and remember can be challenging, but it's worth the effort. In our first few years together, we couldn't afford to take big family vacations. But by packing fun, scrumptious picnic lunches and taking advantage of short trips and excursions within a few hours' driving distance from our home, we were able to eliminate hotel and restaurant bills for our big family. Our excursions included fishing in a friend's pond, exploring a cavern in the northern part of Arkansas, and spending an afternoon on the lake with friends in their boat. With a little imagination, a big family can have fun together without spending a lot of money or traveling far from home. Recording the fun on film provides a lasting "memorial" to be relived over and over again if pictures are placed in an accessible photo album. Remember, kids are natural-born hams, and they love seeing themselves in pictures.

BIRTHDAY BASHES

My best friend thinks we overdo our family birthdays, and she is probably right. We do go a little overboard, but there is a good reason for it. Obviously, neither Harvey nor I were around when our stepchildren were born. A stepparent doesn't have the same bond with their stepchild as they do with their own child. We certainly want to love them as we do our own, but that relationship has to develop with time and effort. One way Harvey and I found to solidify this bond and strengthen our family knot is by giving everyone their special day of celebration, gifts, and surprises on their birthday. The whole family gets in on the fun. The objective, of course, is to make the birthday person feel as if the world revolves around him or her for this one day out of the year.

I have been called the Queen of Theme. Every bash has a theme. We had a hippie party for Mandi's fourteenth birthday, a horse party for Sara's fifteenth, a musical party for Aaron's sixteenth, and a grown-up rose party for Jennifer's seventeenth. We have gone bowling, go-carting, and shopping. Over the years, no one has ever had a dull birthday because in our "family" we want every member to know they belong.

ME, A MINIVAN MOM?

Who would have ever thought—me, a minivan mom? Actually, after my divorce I had my life planned out. I thought that by age forty I would be able to have fun doing things for myself. I thought about going back to school or just furthering myself as a career woman. My kids would be older, and I would have a lot of free time. All those plans changed when I married Harvey. He was a package deal. He came with three daughters, all of whom were younger than my own children.

Once word gets out to a teacher that you are a stay-at-home mom and you have a minivan, it's all over. You can expect the children's teachers to fight over whose turn it is to have you accompany their class on the next field trip. The stay-at-home status is only a figment of someone's imagination. Apart from the school field trips, there was scouts, piano lessons, art lessons, horseback riding lessons, ball games, cheerleading, and school plays. I feel sure there were other activities that added miles to our poor old minivan's odometer, but they escape me for now.

What doesn't escape me is the family bond that was achieved in those endless hours of driving from one activity to the next. Naturally, we had our aggravated assaults in the back of the van, but there were also times of congratulations over a good game and sincere condolences over a bad one. Believe it or not, that old minivan is still around. We've named it Clifford, after the big red dog. No one wants to drive it anymore, but it holds a lot of family memories.

Doing things together as a family is critical to blending. If our children see that they mean enough to us to cause us to want to cart them all over creation and back, they also will see that they belong to the family. If we do this job begrudgingly or not at all, our children will see those attitudes and feel that they don't belong. Of course, our children don't recognize all the things we do for them until much later, usually after they have moved out on their own. One evening while visiting at home, Jennifer shared with us how much it meant to her that we were always there for her. Each of our six children has said the same thing at different times over the last few years.

It amazes me how what used to be the most unappreciated thing I did as a mom has now become my own personal treasure trove of great memories!

HOLIDAYS

The melding of two families' traditions into the *new* family's tradition is especially difficult during the holidays. Most of the fondest memories we and our children hold are of family holiday times. Unfortunately, in the blended family the fond memories and traditions can drive wedges if not handled thoughtfully and carefully.

Holidays leave a bittersweet taste for everyone in the blended family. We love the festivities, food, and fun that accompany the holidays; but visitation, separations, and changes in the way we have always done our celebrating dampen them.

One of my stepdaughters shared with me recently how much she used to hate the holidays. Even though our family did all we could to make the times meaningful and special, our kids still had to split their time between two households. They hated missing Christmas morning in one household or having to eat two Thanksgiving dinners. As parents, we plan the holidays around our family—our kids. When we have to leave in the middle of the day to pick up the kids or plan a meal around their late arrival or early departure, our plans become complicated. Attitudes tend to need some adjustment at those times.

Visitation agreements increase the stress and tension in blended families. Harvey and I found that by letting go of our planned program and set traditions, we were able to create an atmosphere of peaceful celebration when the children were with us. This made our holidays more memorable.

Sometimes old traditions can be carried over into the new blended family, but sometimes it is better to let them go. Picture this scenario: A child who always got the job of placing the star at the top of the Christmas tree is anxious to finish the decorating so he can perform his duty. Then the unthinkable happens—an angel that has been in his new stepmother's family for generations replaces the all-important star. Because of its fragile condition, she insists on placing it at the top of the tree herself. Both stepmother and stepchild feel threatened, and dad is in the middle—he can't win. A wedge has been driven into the new and delicate relationship between stepchild and parent. This scenario is typical of the small straws that build upon the camel's back and eventually break up a marriage.

In this make-believe scenario, we can see that this is where the parents must remember their "vision" of the completed house. Here is an example of how closed-door communication and obedience to Christ as the foundation of the home are key to building a strong family. Talking through this situation, weighing the importance of our old way of doing things against having a solid family, can actually result in creating new traditions. In our make-believe family, mom and dad may decide to have two Christmas trees—one topped with an angel and the other with a star. Or maybe the angel will receive a new place of honor on the mantle. Maintaining peace in the home while remembering the reason for celebration should remain our focus.

Our goal was for everyone in the family to have a great Christmas holiday. In my own family, we did several things to compromise and compensate for the two-family Christmas situation. One compromise that immediately comes to mind happened a few days before our first Christmas as a family. Harvey's two younger daughters came to me in secret. They whispered that I had to put out a jar of pickles for Mandi to find on Christmas morning because she would be really disappointed if she got up and didn't find them. My confusion over this odd tradition led me to ask Harvey about it because I didn't want Mandi to feel jilted over pickles. Behind closed doors, Harvey explained that Mandi loved pickles, and her mother loved to surprise her with a whole jar on Christmas morning. This was a unique and special tradition between Mandi and her mother; therefore, we decided we would not intrude on it.

One Christmas tradition I brought with me, much to all of the children's dismay, is the reading of the Christmas story on Christmas morning—*before* the presents are opened. Everyone in the family hates it. They dread having to sit through the story in the second chapter of Luke while staring at all the gifts spilling out from under the tree. I don't know if anyone even listens to the Bible reading, but they are all reminded of the -reason for the season.

My children and stepchildren alike became united in their efforts to prevent the delay in opening their gifts. One year, Sara, Harvey's middle daughter, hid all of the Bibles in the house. Her efforts only delayed the Bible reading and gift opening until I found an old King James Version Bible she overlooked. One of the most creative delay tactics came from my daughter Jennifer. When the family gathered in the living room around the tree, she presented to me a beautiful glass snowball with a Nativity scene inside. The unique thing about this lovely snowball was that it told the Christmas story when you wound it up—that year they heard it twice! Another year, Aaron, my sixteen-year-old eccentric son, offered to read the story for me. Of course I was thrilled that one of the kids finally took an interest in this very important part of our Christmas morning. Aaron began his "reading" with all of the "a-hems" to collect everyone's attention. His paraphrased version began with "Jesus" and ended with "was born"—and nothing else in between. Nice try.

Reading the Christmas story on Christmas morning has become a Clark family tradition. Though it was once dreaded, it is now expected. Everyone knows that once Jesus has been acknowledged and we have prayed together as a family, the chaos of opening gifts amid loud talking, thank-yous, and torn wrapping paper can begin.

Church, Not an Option

People have asked me where Harvey and I met. I always tell them: "The third row on the left side." I usually don't have to give any other explanations because most of us are creatures of habit. I always sat in the third row on the left side in church. Of course Harvey said he noticed me a few months before—when I was dressed in a laundry basket with socks pinned in my hair for a harvest festival our church was giving for the children. I was working the bowling game with that silly basket around my waist. Can you imagine being attracted to a basket of dirty laundry?

Church has been an important part of my life since my salvation in the early '70s. I don't know where I would be if it had not been for the balanced Bible teaching and the love of Christ demonstrated through the body of Christ. Through the depression and pain of my divorce, I sought spiritual strength, encouragement, and comfort in church. My children and I found the stability and support we so desperately needed in the fellowship of believers.

Harvey, too, sought the Lord when his life was falling apart around him. The words of his mother were still ringing in his ears. She said, "Boy, you either be hot or you be cold . . . 'cause if you're gonna be lukewarm, God will speeeww you out of his mouth!" Harvey had been living his life "cold," but he knew it was time to get serious with God. He went to church looking for fuel to flame his newly kindled fire.

Our relationship began in church. There was never a question about whether we would bring our children to church. Church was not an option. Don't get me wrong—it wasn't always an easy ride in our minivan. Remember, in a blended family one must contend with outside influences.

In a biological family, there are the normal trials and friends that pull your kids away from the way you are trying to rear them. In a blended family, it could be the child's own mother or father in the other household who tells them they can worship God at home. They don't have to go to church when they are at that parent's house, so what's the big deal about going to church when they are back home with you?

Setting a standard in your blended family is kind of like selling a car. You don't say how much you want for it and then try to go *up* in price when you see that the buyer is interested. Because you know the value of the car, you determine ahead of time what you will take for it—then you set your price higher, based on the car's value. This may bring you the full value price, but it also allows room for you to come down—without compromising on the amount you will take. Both buyer and seller leave happy.

In a blended family, we set our standards high as well. Harvey and I determined early on what we would allow. Attending church was never optional. Every Sunday everyone got ready to go. However, when our girls began to protest about wearing dresses to church, we "came down in price," allowing them to wear nice, clean pants. This was a hard one for me because I always felt that on Sundays we should give God our best—including our dress. God gently showed me that our daughters were more receptive to hearing his Word if they were happy in their pants rather than angry in a dress. (Funny how things change—now they *want* to wear dresses to church.)

Every marriage and family is different, with different circumstances and influences. We must factor in our children's ages, past history, and whether they are living with us full-time or part-time. We want the time we spend with our children to have a positive influence on them, not be a negative time of continual conflict. I have found a lot of wisdom in the book of Proverbs. Solomon's familiar words in Proverbs 22:6 instruct us to "train up a child in the way he should go." This is our responsibility and a charge from God. The "way *we* should go" is more than just forcing our children to go to church with us on Sunday. It is living an exemplary life by being an example for them to follow and showing them—through our actions and attitudes—that we love them unconditionally. The promise attached to this proverb is, "and when he is old, he will not depart from it."

I can't help but chuckle when I read this promise because now that our children are grown, they actually *expect* the Bible reading on Christmas morning, and they *love* dressing up for church. Harvey and I tied our family knot together by trying to provide everyone with a sense of belonging. Our consistency, although detested at times, later translated itself into stability and love.

Ol' Rudolph still watches over the mantle where all the stockings hang as a memorial to our sons and daughters. You can almost hear him whispering, "Look what God has done."

Chapter Five

SNAKE EGGS AND HAM: THE STEPPARENT-STEPCHILD POWER STRUGGLE

The heart is more deceitful than all else and is desperately sick;
Who can understand it? I, the LORD, search the heart.
~ Jeremiah 17:9–10a

*L*ike the Dr. Suess character in the book *Green Eggs and Ham,*[1] we want to say, "I do not like them Sam I Am!" It doesn't take a stepparent long to discover that he or she really doesn't want to try this new dish being served up. Power struggles between stepparent and stepchild are one of the most explosive issues in the blended family.

At the risk of looking like the wicked stepmother from my children's fairy-tale stories, I want to give you a glimpse into the dark side of my heart (the side I'd rather keep hidden) in order to show you that all of us have this potential. The Bible says in Jeremiah 17:9–10, "The heart is more deceitful than all else and is desperately sick; Who can understand it? I, the LORD, search the heart, I test the mind, even to give to each man according to his ways, according to the results of his deeds."

How deceitful is the heart? We can be deceived into believing we are doing good when, in all honesty, we are desperately sick in our words and actions. Only by allowing a loving and patient God to search our hearts and test our minds will we see the resulting damage of living life selfishly and demanding our own way.

Having been a Christian for several years before I married Harvey, I had a pretty good handle on being a Christian—I thought. After a few years of blending, however, I found out there were things down inside of me that I never knew existed. Instead of securely tying my family knot, I was tying my poor family *into* knots.

I was in a continual state of anger, overreacting to many of the little things my stepchildren did. I seemed to have an ax to grind, and they were my grinding stone. My little ax became sharper and sharper until finally, after splitting every hair on every head, I became so frustrated and disgusted with myself, I cried out to God for help.

SNAKE EGGS

Our morning began as any other. All five of the kids were lined up on the kitchen bar stools eating their breakfast while I was on the opposite side packing lunches. A glance at the clock made me quicken my pace. The school in town was twenty miles away. I knew we would have to leave in the next ten minutes or everyone would be late. School traffic on the two-lane highway was always maddening in the mornings. As I hurried out the door and loaded kids, backpacks, lunches, and school projects into the van, a quick headcount told me Sara was missing.

If I were to characterize our daughter Sara, the most fitting description would be Ellie Mae from the TV series *The Beverly Hillbillies.* At the time Sara was in the fifth grade. She was a delightful child—always smiling and a tomboy through and through. Like the Ellie Mae character, Sara loved critters—she still does. She loved puppies, frogs, crawdads, caterpillars, and any living creature that happened to cross her path. (After the time I pulled out a bunch of dead, fuzzy caterpillars that had been squished and forgotten, I learned never to stick my hands in her pockets on laundry day. She had to empty her own -pockets after that.) In addition to Sara's love for animals and crawly critters, she had a tendency to be late, disheveled, and forgetful. So when Sara turned up missing in the van that morning, it was no surprise.

I started the van and went back into the house to find Sara. She ran past me with her right arm behind her back. Before she could climb into the van, I asked her what she was hiding. She responded, "Nothing." The shoebox peeking out from behind her back looked rather suspicious, so I pressed her a little further by asking what was in the box. She said, "Nothing, just something for Mrs. Mayfield's class." Her classroom had a special science room for students to display pets and other interesting projects with the class. Sara was always finding things in nature to share with the class, so this wasn't unusual. However, she had never tried to hide them from me.

Knowing Sara, the contents of the box could be anything. I demanded to see inside, so she slowly, carefully lifted the lid. Sara said it was a box of dirt, and that is exactly what it looked like at first. Confident that the box concealed something more sinister than dirt, I picked up a stick and poked around. Sara squirmed when a little cluster of white snake eggs peaked out from beneath the soil. My face reddened as visions of children being bitten by baby rattlesnakes or copperhead snakes raced through my mind. I told Sara that she could not take the snake eggs to school until her dad could examine them and assure me that there was no danger.

In defiance, Sara grabbed the box out of my hands and said: "I'm taking these eggs to school! You're not my mother, and I don't care what you say." My stress level was climbing as I gripped the other end of the box and proceeded to tell her, "No, you're not!" With Sara and I each holding onto the ends of the box, the tug-of-war was on. We pulled back and forth until I finally took the box from Sara and tossed it on the table. We both angrily climbed into the van and headed toward town.

The argument escalated as we drove down the highway—the more Sara defied my authority, the angrier I became. The angrier I became, the heavier my foot pushed on the gas pedal. I happened to look down at my speedometer and was startled to see that I was going nearly 80 mph! I let off the gas and began to slow down— then I noticed the flashing blue lights reflected in my rearview mirror. The policeman had clocked me at 72 mph. This was a true case of road rage. Making matters worse, I recognized the policeman. I had recently processed his home loan at the mortgage company where I worked (one of the benefits of living in a small community).

Embarrassed and in tears, I tried to explain the snake egg argument and being late for school. Sympathetic, but unmoved, the officer handed me my ticket and told me to slow down. As I sat on the side of the road trying to gain my composure before pulling out again, I thought to myself, *It's not even seven o'clock yet; how could this morning possibly get any worse?* Then, as if to answer my unspoken question, Mandi broke the silence by asking, "Terri, do you know you have your shirt on inside-out?"

CONTROL ISSUES

Mine and Sara's tug-of-war wasn't about gaining control over a box of snake eggs. Our struggle went deeper. As a stepmother, I was pulling hard for respect and acknowledgment of my parental authority; and Sara was pulling just as hard to keep from giving it to me.

Like many other blended families, we had a lot of control issues and power struggles. These struggles pop up everywhere between everyone. Ours seemed to go through a rotation. One day the struggle would be between me and my stepchildren; the next time, between my husband and my children. Another day, the argument would be between Harvey and me or between both sets of children.

Behavior influenced by divorce triggers resentments in all of us. I was holding all of the confrontations and irritations with my husband's ex-wife in unforgiveness. By transferring my frustrations onto my stepchildren, I felt as if I was in control. In truth, I was being controlled by my unforgiveness.

Sara's resentments stemmed from a loyalty to her mother. Many children of divorce—even children who have lost a parent to death—experience this sense of loyalty. She was afraid that if she acknowledged my authority or if she got close to me, she would be betraying her mother. Knowing the source of these resentments, however, doesn't excuse responsible adults from acting like responsible adults—especially responsible *Christian* adults.

JUSTIFIED BY FATE

Being the adult, I felt perfectly justified in telling Sara she couldn't take her snake eggs to school. However, under the surface, where no one but God sees, I knew I was being too harsh with Sara. Resentments from previous challenges and confrontations were furrowing around in my heart, clouding my judgment. I told myself and everyone else that the snake eggs posed a danger to Mrs. Mayfield's class. This justification, though, had no merit. My reaction to Sara was based upon past offenses—resentments she had toward me—and my mood. In fact, it wouldn't have mattered if she had been perfectly up-front about the snake eggs; I would have said no anyway. Sara knew this, and that's why she tried to sneak them past me.

Saying no to Sara and asserting my authority made me feel that I had won the power struggle tug-of-war. In actuality, however, no one wins this kind of game. God and I both knew my marriage, my children, and my stepchildren were all suffering as a result of my anger. Outwardly, I was able to go to church, worship God, love other people, teach, and be a good wife and mother, but as soon as one of my stepchildren stepped out of line—look out! Sometimes it was nothing more than a rolling of the eyes when I told them to do something. It didn't take much.

MUDBUGS AND RESENTMENTS

In Arkansas we have little lobsterlike critters known as crawfish. We call them crawdads, or mudbugs. They live underground where the soil is moist. As these little guys furrow their way around the yard, they push dirt to the surface. The dirt they push up out of their way forms little mounds resembling tiny volcanoes. When the ground is wet, our yard becomes littered with these little mudbug mounds. Walking on mudbug-infested ground is like walking on a wet sponge; the furrowed holes just below the surface fill with water, making the ground soft and squishy.

Like the mudbugs living in our yard, resentments can multiply just below the surface without us noticing them. The many mounds they leave behind, however, are evidence to everyone that they exist.

My heart was infested by these mudbuglike resentments. The evidence I was leaving behind were the eruptions of my temper—little volcanoes. Yes, Sara had her share of resentments, too; but I was the adult, and she was the child. The responsibility of digging up those nasty little mudbugs was on me. Ignoring them and allowing them to multiply made my family very unstable.

The snake-egg incident would have gone much better if I had taken control of the resentments building in me. If I hadn't permitted this lethal button to exist, Sara couldn't have pushed it. As it was, I was an eruption waiting to happen.

Hindsight is always 20/20, so here is how I think the same snake-egg scenario would have played out minus the resentments inside me. Without the resentments, I probably would have told Sara that we could take the box into the school and show Mrs. Mayfield the eggs. If Mrs. Mayfield felt uncomfortable about leaving them there, I would have taken them back home.

Without my resentments, Sara would not have felt the need to defy or challenge me. Without her defiance and challenges, I surely wouldn't have gotten a ticket that morning. In fact, the worst part of that morning could have been discovering my shirt was on inside-out.

You may be feeling some of these same ugly emotions toward your stepchildren. If you are, then I want to encourage you with hope. Overcoming resentments is not only possible, but we can actually have great relationships with our step-children as well.

The question remains: How do you identify *and* rid yourself of resentments before they multiply and infest your family? Identifying my resentments really wasn't very difficult—the rise in blood pressure was a pretty good indication of their presence. Acknowledging that part of the problem was in *me* was another matter altogether. Since the Garden of Eden, pointing blame at someone else has been the nature of man and woman.

In my case, I pointed the blame at my stepdaughters' defiance and disrespect, at my husband's ex-wife, and even at my husband for being too lenient with the girls when they needed to be disciplined. I dug up old offenses as well as differences in the way he dealt with my children and his. All in all, I was worn out—emotionally, physically, and spiritually.

SAYING YES

Finally reaching my saturation point, I called a friend to cry on her shoulder. I told her all about the snake eggs and my ticket, blubbering on and on about the problems I was having with my stepchildren. After patiently enduring my cries and complaints, she made a suggestion: Look for things to say *yes* to. In other words, when Mandi, Sara, or Jodie asked permission to do something, she wanted me to examine their request to see if I could give them approval. My friend was asking me to *look* for opportunities to extend grace—unmerited favor.

This became a real turning point for me because it caused me to examine my motives for saying no. I realized I was saying no far more than I was saying yes. Most of the time I simply didn't *want* to give to them what they wanted.

I had permitted resentments to build up in me over a period of two or three years. Saying no to the girls became my way of asserting my authority as their stepmother because they weren't respecting me as a parent. The resentments building in me were actually unforgiven offenses. Granted, some of the offenses were deserving of discipline; but once the discipline had taken place, it should have been over. Instead, somewhere in the back of my heart, I stored them up—one offense on top of another. These little "mudbugs" were eroding my family.

In order to extend grace to my stepchildren, I had to forgive them, and in order to forgive them, I had to come to a turning point. I call this turning point "repentance." The *heart* of repentance is to be truly sorry for your sin and want to change. The *act* of repentance is recognizing that you are going the wrong way, stopping, and then turning around and going in the right direction. Although feeling sorry for our sin is critical, it isn't enough to change us. We must make a conscience decision to stop what we are doing wrong and begin doing what is right.

Jesus demonstrated grace toward us when he willingly gave up his life on the cross. He didn't deserve the floggings or the insults, much less the cruel death he endured when he was crucified. He lived the perfect sinless life. Jesus didn't deserve the punishment of death on the cross—I did. God reminded me of the fact that we all stand guilty of offending him in our sin. Yet even though we're sinners, his grace is extended to us daily. So who was I to stand in judgment over anyone else, particularly a child? I needed not only to lay the offenses received from my stepchildren down, but I needed to lay *my own* sin and offenses at the cross as well.

None of this was easy. The little mudbugs of resentment and unforgiveness had a grip on me, but worse, I held an even tighter grip on them. Jesus had to pry my fingers off of them because I didn't *want* to let go. In our day-to-day lives, we tend to excuse and pass over sin in ourselves, especially when it means we must admit we're wrong. Repenting and turning gave me a fresh new look at my stepchildren. As my friend suggested, I began looking for opportunities to say *yes*.

YES, LORD

Before I could say yes to my stepchildren, I had to begin by saying yes to God. As Christians, we learn early on that God expects us to walk by a higher standard: "From everyone who has been given much, much will be required" (Luke 12:48). The other side of that coin is knowing that whatever God asks us to do, we can do it through his strength instead of relying on our own wisdom, strength, or abilities (Phil. 4:13). This comforting knowledge gave me the push I needed to say yes to God.

I began by taking just one small request at a time. For example, when Jodie asked for a second helping of ice cream in the evening, typically I would give an automatic no. But after I prayed and asked God to help me with these resentments, I took a different approach. Checking my motives, I looked at the clock to see how late in the evening it was to be eating sugar and then decided an extra helping wouldn't hurt anything. You should have seen the kids' faces when I said yes—all five jumped up and made a mad dash for the kitchen and a second helping of ice cream.

Little by little—one whispered prayer at a time—God began to change my heart. As my heart softened toward the girls, I realized that my stepdaughters were becoming more respectful of me. They were approaching me with their needs more often because I was becoming more approachable. Amazing!

My dad used to say, "Respect is earned." I wanted my stepchildren to respect me. Setting a standard for everyone in the family to live by was easy, but somehow I missed setting it for myself. God showed me that I was expecting to receive what I was unwilling to give. I was trying to be a good mom by -packing great lunches, being involved in school and extra-curricular activities, decorating the kids bedrooms to suit each one's personality, making a good "sit down at the table" dinner every night, helping with homework, etc.

Because I was doing all the outward things, I thought I *deserved* respect. However, I was holding on to too much resentment to do those things from a pure heart. The more I *did,* the more I *expected;* the less I *received,* the more I *resented.* It was a vicious circle. This cycle was finally broken when I humbled myself in repentance.

I Do Like Them, Sam I Am!

In the Dr. Suess story *Green Eggs and Ham,* Sam's finicky, yellow friend is hounded over and over to try green eggs and ham. He insists he does not like green eggs and ham, but he has never actually tasted them. After Sam's relentless efforts to convince him he will love them if he just tries them, he finally gives in and takes a bite. The expression on his face and the declaration that follows prove that you can't judge by appearances. He indeed loved those green eggs—once he tried them. The key was trying them.

Have you ever tried to convince a five-year-old to eat something green? Forget it. Unless you force it down their throats, they won't eat it. With this in mind, think of yourself as those green eggs and ham in your stepchild's eyes. In the blended family, power struggles often surface because our stepchildren decide right away that they don't like us. We do all we can to get them to appreciate us—after all, *we* know we are nice people, so why can't they see it?

In our zeal to jump in and make our families come together, we can make costly mistakes. These mistakes can damage relationships with our children for many years. To give you an example, I know a young man whose mother died when he was a boy. Later, when his father remarried, his father and stepmother insisted that he call his stepmother Mom. The boy was still grieving the loss of his mother. In his mind, they were telling him that his stepmother was replacing his mother. This young man told me that he resented his father and his stepmother for years. He felt as though he not only lost his mother, but he lost his dad as well. This mistake resulted in a power struggle that lasted several years.

Stepparents do not have the same blood bond as the biological parent. We bear the name "parent" and its responsibility, but love between stepchild and stepparent grows as any relationship grows—with time, trust, and communication. Whether you are widowed or divorced, allow some time and patience in blending your family. Don't insist your child eat those green eggs and ham. Over time they will taste your love and learn to appreciate you.

I have the advantage of hindsight now that all of our children are grown and out on their own. Both Harvey and I experienced more than our fair share of the stepparent-stepchild power struggles over the years. Yet we learned through praying, repenting, and obeying God (though sometimes with clenched teeth) to let go of the rope in our power struggle tug-of-war. I now can say with confidence that all of the children we raised in our home love us. They all have come back to say, "I *do* like them, Sam I am."

Chapter Six

NAILING IT DOWN:
COMMUNICATION

"Come now, and let us reason together,"
says the LORD.
~ Isaiah 1:18

*H*arvey did a pretty fair job of holding back the snickers as his six-year-old daughter climbed into the van with her hair all pinned up with bobby pins and clips. She had styled it herself and was quite proud of the way she looked. Jodie's head looked like an overstuffed pin cushion, with bobby pins sticking out in every direction. Strands of beautiful, blond hair were haphazardly twisted, clipped, and pinned—but falling out all over.

Ordinarily, I would just amuse my stepdaughter and praise her efforts to style her own hair, but this visitation evening was different. Harvey had called ahead and told the girls to dress nicely. We had planned to take them to dinner in a nice restaurant and then to the mall to buy new school clothes. This was Jodie's attempt at dressing herself up.

I tried to explain tactfully to Jodie that she would be trying on a lot of clothes. Pulling shirts over her head meant her tresses would have to come down. I showed her the brush I kept in the van, explaining how I would be happy to brush her hair out and fix it for her. Jodie crossed her arms and stuck out her bottom lip, signaling the start of another battle—it was going to be a long night.

Harvey and I hadn't been married very long, and I was still seen by the girls as the wicked stepmother. Jodie wasn't the only one who had walls built around her; in fact, I had a huge fortress of my own. Just being a normal mom was met with resistance, so my suggestion to take her hair down really crossed the line.

Sometimes we stepparents just want to scream, "Why can't we all just get along?!" If we're not settling a fight between the kids, we're settling a complaint from the ex. No sooner do we settle an issue and lay it to rest in one child, when it immediately shows up in another. Old wounds cause insecurities to rear their ugly heads. Rejection from our stepchildren and, sometimes, even our spouse makes us want to run away. The vision that began as a bright, happy home becomes dark and clouded by all the stormy controversies and emotions thundering around us every day. We truly love the person God has brought into our lives—he or she has met every point on our checklist for the perfect spouse. We want to build a solid family, but how do we chase away the dark clouds and realize our vision of a happy home?

The answer is communication. Honest communication is important to any marriage, but in the blended family it is crucial. Communication by definition means *"to impart, share, give or exchange information by talking."* A second definition is *"to have a sympathetic or meaningful relationship; to be connected."* The first definition describes talking; the second takes talking to the next level—connecting.

Once we tie our marital knot, little kinks and tangles begin to emerge. When our children don't respond to our new spouse with love and respect as anticipated, our spouse won't find our kids quite so wonderful. Getting married to someone with children in tow often turns out to be more than we bargained for. Problems with a difficult ex catch us off guard too. We may talk about the problems we are having, but at some point talking about our children or ex isn't enough. We must somehow move our communication level up a notch, from exchanging information and complaining to being connected in a meaningful relationship. Our family and marital bliss depend on it.

As I mentioned in the first chapter, communication can be compared to the nails that hold our house together. If a husband and wife can communicate with each other, any issue can be resolved. This resolution is born out of a mutual trust. We need to trust our spouse with our most treasured possessions—our children—and know our spouse will keep their well-being close at heart.

OLD BAGGAGE

One of the keys to overcoming trust issues is unpacking the "old baggage" we brought with us into our home. We often carry baggage from the past into our new marriage without even realizing it. Baggage comes in many forms, including emotional responses we've packed away from our past marriages and relationships. Though these old garments no longer fit, we drag them around with us just in case we might need them one day.

Why do we stuff our closets with clothes that don't fit anymore or are out of style? Is it because it helps us to retain some semblance of who we used to be? Or maybe we're afraid of feeling alone and vulnerable. We never know when we might need to put on that coat of hard-heartedness or that shirt of defensive self-righteousness.

Old baggage must be unpacked and discarded, one old garment at a time.

Times have changed, and so have our hearts. Throw out that leisure suit of fear, and donate that orange dress of mistrust to the local thrift store. The old shoes of guilt can be thrown in the trash, while that worn-out dress of bitterness can be burned to ashes in the fire of our new love. Old baggage just takes up space in our new homes—space desperately needed for the new garments of healing, restoration, and trust.

Before dad or mom can feel comfortable removing their protective wing from their biological child, they have to feel confident that their new spouse can be trusted with their child. Removing the old baggage and communicating is the first step in trusting our new spouse. Real communication exposes our heart, and once the heart is exposed, it is vulnerable. Scary as this may sound, our vulnerability allows our spouse an opportunity to prove his or her trustworthiness.

A few months after Harvey and I were married, my car broke down. Fearful of his response, I sat in the car for what seemed to be an eternity before finally calling him. I braced myself for the worst before dialing his number. When Harvey answered the phone, I swallowed hard and between apologies and tears I blurted out what had happened.

Harvey had no idea why I was so upset. He kept telling me it was OK; in fact, he acted like he was more worried about me than the car. It never occurred to me that I had carried old baggage into this marriage. I expected him to respond to me according to the experiences of my past. Before I could feel comfortable with Harvey in this area of my life, I had to unpack my old baggage by talking to him and trusting him with my vulnerability. Trust was built a little more each time I let go of my past and called him when I needed him.

Today I never have second thoughts of calling Harvey when I have a car problem, or any other problem for that matter, because he has proven his trustworthiness to me over and over again with his understanding and patience. I have complete confidence that Harvey will respond in a loving and caring way to whatever disaster or calamity in which I find myself. I have unpacked and discarded that old garment of fear and mistrust, replacing it with a new wardrobe of trust.

RESPECT AND CREDIBILITY

A direct result of bonding and developing a trust relationship with your spouse is bonding and developing a relationship with your stepchild. If a parent can't relinquish control over their child to their spouse, how can a stepparent develop any rapport with that child? Kids must see that their mom or dad trusts their stepmom or stepdad.

In a child's eyes a stepparent loses respect and credibility if the child sees his mom or dad arguing with the stepparent for disciplining him or for telling him what to do. For instance, if Harvey tells my daughter Jennifer to empty the dishwasher and I, for some reason, tell her she doesn't have to, Harvey will never be able to get her to do anything around the house again. His authority as a parent will be undermined.

Undermining parental authority is one major reason we should never argue in front of the children. All discussions regarding the kids should be held behind closed doors. In the dishwasher example above, our family will benefit more if I pull Harvey aside and explain to him that Jennifer has three finals to study for; therefore, I would rather empty the dishwasher myself so she can study. He and I can hash through all of our disagreements and reasonings until we are unified in our parenting and reach an agreement. If we agree to release her from the chore, or if we decide she should go ahead and finish the chore first, no argument has occurred in front of the child, and no one's respect has been sacrificed.

Women, especially, have difficulty disciplining their children. Mothering instincts kick in, and we hover over them like a hen with her little chicks. We know our own children better than anyone else does, and we want to protect them because of what they have already been through in their young lives. Because they don't want to see their child hurt again, many mothers are reluctant to allow their new husband to exercise authority over the child.

Men, too, assume a similar but more masculine approach to protecting their child. Dads often handle feelings of guilt over their child's divided life by giving them more attention, time, money, and gifts to compensate for the trauma of divorce and separation. Men tend to want to fix things, making every provision for their child to be secure and happy—conquering all obstacles in their way. Sadly, if they see their new spouse as an obstacle to their child's happiness, they may choose child over spouse, costing them their new marriage.

In a single-parent home, we often skew our parenting to make up for the pain of divorce, separation, and the hardship of parenting alone. When we remarry, we need our spouse's input and counsel to correct these imbalances for the good of the children. Without this communication, we are less like a family and more like a single mom and single dad who live together and share bath towels.

SECRET SIGNALS

Behind closed doors, Harvey and I could discuss anything regarding the children. But what about the times when it's impossible to give a quick answer, or it is obvious that you and your spouse disagree over how to answer the child standing there? Every family gets involved in spur-of-the-moment discussions with their kids. You can't just say, "Hold that thought—we'll be right back," as you run off to the inner sanctum of your room to discuss it. My wise husband, Harvey, devised a secret signal for just this type of situation.

The signal was simply to raise his index finger while looking me in the eye. I did the same if I wanted to signal him. Once the signal was given, the discussion with the kids would be postponed. Harvey would casually wind the conversation down by telling the kids, "Let me think about it, and I'll let you know." This prevented one of us from saying too much or calling down a decision before we could talk about it. The signal also kept the stepparent from being the villain if the answer was not what the child wanted to hear. The kids never knew about our signal or that we talked about everything. As far as they were concerned, Harvey and I simply agreed on all of the decisions.

PARENTING EQUALLY

Parents love to sing their children's praises. If you had the time, I could go on and on about how wonderful my kids are. In fact, I have trouble understanding why others don't see them with the same level of admiration as I do. Naturally, my adoration and love for my kids was carried over into my new marriage, as was Harvey's. Because we loved our own children so much, we assumed we would be able to parent and love our spouse's children with the same enthusiasm. After all, if we had been a good parent to our kids, we would be just as good with our stepchildren, right? Unfortunately, this isn't always the case.

Despite our best intentions, we can easily fall into the trap of unequal parenting if we don't connect with our spouse through open communication. Even in nuclear families, parents parent unequally at times: little brother always gets to stay out later than older sister, or the oldest girl gets new dresses while the younger sister gets the hand-me-downs. In the Bible, favoritism happened as well—look at Jacob and Esau (Gen. 25:28).

Parenting equally is particularly challenging for blended families because parents drag so much baggage with them into a marriage. Couple this with resentments from the stepchildren and conflicts with an ex-spouse, and you've got the makings of an uphill battle.

Parenting both sets of children equally is one of the hardest things to do in a blended family. We *say* we love them all the same, but unless we've had time to bond with them, a real love hasn't had time to take root. Blending a family involves growing a good relationship between all the family members. It doesn't happen instantly when a man and woman say "I do." In some cases it may never happen; but even in those families, parents must look beyond the strained relationships and try to -parent all the children fairly, without prejudice.

I have to admit that when Jodie showed up that night in the van looking like a pin cushion, I didn't have those warm, fuzzy, "Isn't that cute?" feelings of motherly love toward her that I might have had if Jennifer had done the same thing at age six. Today, however, after thirteen years of marriage and blending, I can declare honestly that I love my stepchildren with the same intensity that I love my own birth children. Harvey loves my kids in the same way as well. This love matured over several years of bonding because we've been through a lot together. We have shared memories and experiences, both good and bad. All of our family experiences brought us closer. But regardless of how close we felt toward our children at any given time, we learned to treat everyone fairly and equally.

Not every situation seemed fair to me, but I had to trust my husband. The same trust held for him as well. Our parenting philosophies didn't always agree, but the thing that kept us in unity was our communication. We talked through our disagreements; and if I felt betrayed, I let him know. I had to learn to be open to hearing his explanation because communication goes beyond exchanging two sides of an argument—it includes listening and forgiveness, reasoning together.

Harvey and I "cut our teeth" on one of the most trying tangles of family knot tying—a sixteen-year-old daughter with a car. Because my oldest son had graduated and moved out soon after we married, Jennifer was our first teenager to parent together. Believe me, there is nothing like a sixteen-year-old daughter with a driver's license to break in a new marriage.

Poor Jennifer—she got very few breaks. Enforcing all the rules of the house, we were very strict with her. She was disciplined often by being grounded or losing phone privileges—the two most important things in a teenage girl's life. Jennifer graduated and moved out on her own, but it seemed we were never without a teenage daughter in the house. Mandi took her place in line as the next teenage daughter.

By this time Harvey and I had developed a set of house rules and disciplines that seemed to work fairly well. Because we had been strict with Jennifer and Aaron, I expected the same measure of discipline to apply to Mandi. When it didn't, I became resentful. This is where the "my kid versus your kid" conflicts began to emerge.

As far as I could see, Harvey wasn't parenting fairly. He was parenting his daughter with favoritism. I couldn't understand why he wouldn't discipline Mandi for the same offenses he had disciplined Jennifer. Mandi stayed up past her bedtime talking on the phone, and she rarely came in by her curfew. I was infuriated when Harvey let these infractions slide by with only a mild scolding—the same offenses had cost Jennifer her privileges. It's a good thing the closed-door rule applied in our house because I complained loudly and often. At this point in our blending, I don't think Harvey and I were connecting in our communication.

Communication is a two-sided exchange. Both sides alternately talk and listen. Ideas and concerns are exchanged by both husband and wife—stepparent and parent. I was always great at explaining to Harvey why I didn't like the way he was handling the kids, but I was not so great at listening to his -reason for doing what he did. Like a small child with her hands over her ears, I wasn't listening. I felt betrayed and angry. I had trusted Harvey with my kids, allowing him to discipline them; but now that his daughter was a teen, the rules didn't seem to matter. I wanted to bring the hammer down. I wanted to stomp my foot and yell. It just wasn't fair!

God wanted to remove my stubborn hands from my ears, but I wasn't buying it. Removing my hands would make me vulnerable. Relinquishing control was very uncomfortable for me as a mother and stepmother, but our family needed me to listen to my husband's heart—to trust his judgments concerning both sets of children the same way I trusted him in any other situation. As a result of my stubbornness, a big ugly division arose in our house: I was on one side, and Harvey and Mandi were on the other. Harvey tried to talk to me, but my hands were still over my ears.

Harvey and I needed to get connected on this situation through communication. The only way for that to happen was for me to uncover my ears and first listen to the voice of the Holy Spirit convicting me of my pride and anger. Finally, after wrestling with God for days, I went to Harvey. Right or wrong, we had to come to terms with the situation. Only after surrendering my will to God could I sit down on the bed, behind our closed bedroom door, and really listen to my husband's side of the issue. Once I softened my heart toward Harvey and forgave him, I could actually *hear* what his heart was saying.

Though he seemed to be parenting his children with favoritism, he was actually doing all he could to parent fairly without creating a worse problem between him and his ex-wife or driving a wedge in his relationship with the girls. Harvey had taken all of my concerns to heart, but his biggest concern was that he might lose his daughters if he was too harsh. The threat of their moving out was always present. He felt that minor infractions of the rules dimmed in importance compared to the threat of losing the girls altogether.

Listening to my husband share his fears and concerns gave me a new perspective on our situation. No, I didn't agree with him on his leniency, but I did make a conscious effort to trust him. I realized that my anger and resentment were doing more damage to our family unity than his relaxing of the rules.

WHEAT AND TARES

Jesus told a parable in Matthew 13:24–30 about a farmer who had an enemy. The farmer sowed good seed into his field and then went to bed. While he slept, the enemy came and sowed bad seed, or tares, into the same field. When the wheat began to sprout, the tares came up as well. The workers in the field came to the farmer and asked if they should pull out the tares the enemy had sown. The wise farmer said, "No, lest while you gather up the tares you also uproot the wheat with them" (v. 29 NKJV).

We have an enemy who wants to destroy our family in the same way the farmer's enemy wanted to destroy his field. He creeps in when we are least expecting, so subtly that we may not even notice it is happening. Who is the enemy? The enemy is not our stepchild, spouse, ex, or our spouse's ex. The enemy is Satan. Always crafty, he attempts to destroy our family on two fronts:

- by sowing bad seed (i.e., behavior deserving of discipline) and

- by making us think that pulling out the tares will fix the problem (i.e., insisting on discipline or having our own way).

In our discussions, Harvey and I were in agreement as to what we wanted for all the kids—that every one of them would grow up to be responsible adults who love God. That was and continues to be our prayer for all six of our children. How to reach that goal, however, continued to be a source of contention between us. We did all we could to parent all of our children with consistency and love, sowing the good seed of God's Word and its character-building values into their lives. Good seed was definitely growing in them—right along with the rebellious tares of adolescence.

In our closed-door discussions, we examined all of the issues and circumstances concerning each child and discovered that the circumstances surrounding our two sets of children were completely different. With my children, we never worried about repercussions from their father because he wasn't involved in their lives. Just the opposite was true of the girls' mother. Harvey contended that enforcing rules was less important than losing the girls.

I was ready to yank up those tares as quickly as they cropped up. Harvey, on the other hand, was concerned for the wheat. All the good seed we had sown into the girls' lives would be lost if we lost the girls. Harvey's focus was on the good wheat, while mine was on the bad tares.

Through our communication we finally connected and arrived at a compromise for our teenage tares. Harvey agreed to tighten the reigns and be more of a disciplinarian, while I agreed to look at each infraction of the rules with more sensitivity. I learned to live with some of the tares that were growing up with the wheat. In fact, even in college at age twenty-one and living on her own, Mandi *still* talks on the phone late into the night—but what do I care? She has grown up to be a lovely young woman who loves the Lord.

Trusting our spouse doesn't mean we must simply hand over our child the day we marry and say, "Do with him as you will; I trust you." However, many marriages unravel because trust is *never* established between the parents. If the spouses do not communicate and learn to trust each other with their children, the stepparent remains an outsider, making the family knot impossible to tie. Trust grows as spouses communicate and connect with each other, all the while interacting with the children with sincerity and sensitivity—one step and one day at a time.

Harvey and I didn't argue in front of the kids, but we were never afraid to show our affection for each other. Parents so solid in their love that they can smooch and wink in front of the children (despite the fact that the kids roll their eyes and get grossed out) set an example of how good marriage can be. Affection communicates to our children in a nonverbal way that we love each other as much as we love them. After children have been through the experience of divorce, it is comforting to see that their parent and stepparent are stable in their love for each other.

Today Harvey and I completely trust each other. Our trust grew through communication—by really, really communicating, even when it hurt. God beckons us to come to him with all of our cares and concerns, like a husband beckons his bride: "'Come now, and let us reason together,' says the LORD" (Isa. 1:18). Once we go to God and talk to him about how we feel, "listening" to his Word and Spirit, then reasoning with our spouse will come easier.

At first I was viewed as the wicked stepmother by my stepdaughters; and to a certain degree I probably was. But as Harvey and I reasoned together, I was able to lay aside my harsh demands. Slowly, with time and communication, my walls fell to become a bridge for my stepdaughters to cross. Because I was no longer viewed as the wicked stepmother, they felt welcome to enter the warm castle of my heart.

Chapter Seven

WHO'S THE BOSS?

Nevertheless, each individual among you
also is to love his own wife even as himself,
and the wife must see to it that she respects her husband.
~ Ephesians 5:33

When I was a kid, my big brother was always bossing me around. I dutifully obeyed him until I realized, "Hey! He's just my brother—not my dad!" Armed with this new revelation, I bucked up and said, "I don't have to do what you say 'cause you're not the boss of me!" Of course, I didn't wait around for the headlock and Indian rub that was sure to follow my defiance. It felt good to "stand up" to my big brother, even if I did only stand there for a second.

Have you ever felt that way? None of us likes being bossed around. We'd rather be our own boss, doing things our own way. Coming under someone else's authority or having to answer to another person isn't an easy thing to do, especially if we are used to doing things our own way.

77

Almost as soon as we say "I do" in our blended family marriage, "who's the boss?" issues begin to surface, and cracks form before the foundational cement has even had time to set. Preexisting circumstances and parent-child authority issues put a strain on unsuspecting newlyweds. Left unchecked, these issues can play a major role in weakening the marriage. When you find these cracks in your foundation, follow them to where they begin and then repair them.

Many who marry into a blended family situation have trouble drawing new lines of authority in their homes. The answer isn't always as cut-and-dried as you might think. Consider the single mom who has been the sole authority figure over her child for several years. When she marries, mom suddenly changes positions from head of the house to wife, helpmate, and second-in-command. Does she relinquish her position of authority over her child? How will her child respond to a change in command? How much control does she give her new husband? Does she have the final say in matters concerning her child? Is she still the boss?

What about the part-time dad whose kids live with his ex-wife. Because of the short time he gets to spend with them and the guilt that brings, he lets them have a little more free rein. He takes them to fun, exciting places and buys them more ice cream than they usually get at home. After marrying, he changes positions from being a fun, part-time dad to being the head of his new household, a full-time husband, and a father to his stepchildren. How much, if any, does he change in his visits with his own kids? How does he go from being in full control of all he does and spends to being accountable to a wife and kids? Is he still the boss?

ORDER OF AUTHORITY

God designed the family with an order of authority. Every member of the family has a responsibility to fulfill their place in that order. When we step outside of God's order and do things our own way, the whole family suffers the consequences. If we parents don't respect each other, how can we expect our children to respect their stepparent? When we humble ourselves, building our home by God's design, our marriage and family will hold together because husband, wife, and God are in unity. Ecclesiastes 4:12 says, "A cord of three strands is not quickly torn apart."

In a blended family, tying these strands together into a family knot is a little trickier than in a first marriage where no children are involved. Still, the blueprint drafted by God for a solid marriage and home can be achieved through sensitivity and patience. The key element to God's design is his order of authority: Christ is the head over the man; the man is the head of his household and the covering over his wife; and the wife is the husband's helper, counselor, and friend.

Adhering to contemporary thought leads to the compromising of our home's foundation. We might as well skimp on the concrete or pour it only halfway if we want to build it by the world's standards. However, if we want a solid family to endure through all of life's storms, we have to build it by God's design. God's Word clearly states that he first wants us to have a relationship with him, thereby laying a solid foundation. Once we submit ourselves to him, then we submit ourselves to one another in love. Ephesians 5:22–31 spells it out very plainly for us:

> Wives, be subject to your own husbands, as to the Lord. For the husband is the head of the wife, as Christ also is the head of the church, He Himself being the Savior of the body. But as the church is subject to Christ, so also the wives ought to be to their husbands in everything.

> Husbands, love your wives, just as Christ also loved the church and gave Himself up for her, so that He might

sanctify her, having cleansed her by the washing of water with the word, that He might present to Himself the church in all her glory, having no spot or wrinkle or any such thing; but that she would be holy and blameless. So husbands ought also to love their own wives as their own bodies. He who loves his own wife loves himself; for no one ever hated his own flesh, but nourishes and cherishes it, just as Christ also does the church, because we are members of His body. For this reason a man shall leave his Father and mother and shall be joined to his wife, and the two shall become one flesh.

In addition to laying out the order of authority, the Bible is also clear on how a husband and wife are to behave toward each other. A man is to love his wife as Christ loves the church, and the wife is to respect and support her husband. In the marriage covenant, the buck has to stop somewhere. Final decisions on issues affecting the family must be someone's ultimate responsibility. According to God's design, the buck stops at the husband's feet. The wife offers her counsel, opinions, and prayers, then respectfully submits her will and trust to her husband for the final decision concerning herself and her family.

DIVINE DESIGN

"Newsflash: Men and women are created different!" Now there's an understatement for you. Of course we all have our own personalities, quirks, and moods; but overall, men and women think and respond differently to just about everything. This is by design. One is not above the other; man and woman go together like salt and pepper, complementing and enhancing the whole blended stew. God created man and woman to uniquely complete each other and yet remain completely unique. Though tasting the hot and spicy ingredients that go into blending a family may leave us a little breathless, it can be swallowed without resulting in "heart" burn if we follow God's design for order of authority in the home.

The roles men and women play in marriage are very different. God defines those roles in his Word by saying that the man is to be the "head," or protector, over a woman, and the woman is to be the "helper," or supporter, for the man (Eph. 5:23 and Gen. 2:18). Men tend to be more logical, and women lean toward the emotional.

To illustrate a man's logical tendency and a woman's emotional tendency, I'll use my husband and myself as an example. On a cross-country road trip to visit my family, I asked Harvey a question. I don't even remember the question now, but after I asked it, he just kept on driving, looking straight ahead and acting as if I wasn't even in the car. I knew he heard me, so I thought he was rudely ignoring me.

Unable to think of a good reason for Harvey to ignore me, I assumed that he must be mad about something. I thought about all the conversations we had had in the car from the time we left Arkansas all the way to the desert roads we were crossing in New Mexico. I couldn't think of a single thing that would have made him clam up like that. Once I determined that there was absolutely nothing for him to be mad about, the tables turned, and I got mad.

I sat there for a full ten minutes stewing, waiting for Harvey to answer me, getting angrier with each passing mile and each digital tick on the dashboard clock. Then, just when I couldn't contain my tongue any longer, he spoke. Calmly and logically, oblivious to my rising blood pressure, Harvey gave me an answer to the question I had asked him, oh so long ago.

While I was getting emotional, thinking that Harvey was ignoring me, he actually had been processing. Taking my question seriously, he had been turning it over and over in his mind, looking at it from every angle. After ten minutes of examining the question thoroughly, he came up with a very sound response. I was speechless! It never occurred to me that he was thinking about what I asked him.

Harvey processes all the time. After thirteen years, I'm finally getting used to it. I have come to realize that a man's way of pondering before he answers is God's way of building a protective covering for a family. In Proverbs 15:28, it says, "The heart of the righteous ponders how to answer." This makes me wonder if I process facts long enough because I always have a quick answer for everything—just ask me!

The fact that men and women respond differently doesn't make men better than women. On the contrary, God created men and women different so that they would complement and complete each other—loving and serving each other, interacting as Christ and his bride the church.

COMPLEMENT AND COMPLETE

When God's design is not followed, instead of complementing and completing each other, a husband and wife end up contending and competing with each other. When a husband and wife are living for themselves rather than for God and each other, a door is opened for Satan to bring destruction into their home. Most marriages in blended families fall apart because they refuse to submit themselves to God's order of authority and his design for marriage.

Believe it or not, God had a reason for making man the head over the woman to have authority over her. He also had a reason for putting the woman in submission to her husband to respect his authority. Paul reminds us in 1 Timothy 2:14 that it was not Adam who was deceived, but the woman. I sometimes wonder if the same fate would have befallen mankind if Satan had approached Adam instead of Eve. Satan had plenty of opportunity to do so before God created Eve. Would Adam have processed the situation as Harvey did, only to decide against taking the fruit?

By God's design, a man will process a situation before giving an answer. A woman is designed to respond faster. If I took as long as my husband to make a decision, nothing would ever get done! Is it any wonder women are such great multitaskers?

This is not to say that women can't make good decisions or think for themselves. On the contrary, Proverbs 31:10–31 describes a woman of excellence or an excellent wife. She was a great businesswoman who made a lot of sound decisions benefiting both her husband and her family. A wise woman who works hard taking care of her family is to be commended.

God isn't looking for men to rule over their wives with an iron fist or for women to be insignificant servants for the husbands to boss around. Imbalance of authority is completely out of God's character and design. Woman was created to be man's counterpart. God's Word is very clear on how the man is to behave toward his wife and that he should respect her. Christ, himself, is our example. Christ, the Bridegroom, loves the church, his bride. He died and gave himself for her. The bride of Christ looks to him as her head and is subject to him (see Eph. 5:24).

A WIFE'S COUNSEL

Because of the way God designed women, a wife's counsel is invaluable to her husband. She sees past the facts of a situation and into the heart. She usually considers how a decision will affect a child emotionally, offering a feminine angle to the overall picture. Normally, after discussing and exploring all sides of a situation, a husband and wife can reach an agreement without needing to address the submission issue. There are, however, times when an agreement cannot be reached. Hard as this might be to accept, a wife is obligated to submit at this point. If her husband makes the wrong choice and it hurts the family, he is accountable to God, not his wife.

I am a rather stubborn woman, especially when it comes to my children, but God was persistent in his mercy, showing me that I didn't always have to be right. Proverbs 14:1 finally got my attention, saying: "The wise woman builds her house, but the foolish tears it down with her own hands." This was hard for me to accept, but God showed me that even if I was right and Harvey was wrong, the ultimate responsibility was upon his shoulders because he was the head of our home. I didn't even have the right to shake my finger at Harvey and say, "I told you so!"

God prefers humility and obedience over being right. What does he require of us? According to Micah 6:8, it is to do justice, love kindness, and to walk humbly with our God. This revelation, though slow in coming, revolutionized my walk with God, my marriage, my relationship with my children, and our family as a whole.

God truly blessed me every time I chose to swallow my pride in submission. I found that the world didn't come to a screeching halt because things weren't done the right (my) way. I also discovered that my husband was more willing to listen to me when I was willing to let him make the final decision. Our family experienced less tension when we followed the basic rules of God's order of authority in our home. The children were more accepting of both my and my husband's authority over them because they knew we were in unity.

A husband and wife who are obedient to God, following his design for their marriage, are building their home on a solid foundation. A wife, in her stubbornness, may think she is doing the best thing for her family by demanding her way. Regardless of whether she is right or wrong, in actuality her stubbornness and disobedience cause cracks to form in her home's foundation, weakening her family structure. The same is true of a -husband who makes decisions without considering his wife's counsel. His disregard for his helpmate is like pouring a concrete foundation without reinforcement bars. It won't hold together, and cracks immediately appear under the weight of the house.

BASIC RULES TO FOLLOW

The obvious question is: How? How does a woman who has been the only parent to her children let go? How does a man who has never been a full-time parent take the headship in his home? How do the children come to accept this new authority that has been placed over them? Because each family scenario has its own history and emotional attachments, there are no simple answers to these and countless other questions. However, if we follow a few basic rules, any family can resolve authority issues peacefully.

Bringing our family under God's rule of authority wasn't easy for Harvey and me because my children didn't want to accept a "new" dad. Harvey is a big guy, an ex-cop with a deep voice—his very presence is intimidating. My children discovered that pulling the wool over Harvey's eyes was next to -impossible. They liked it when it was just me and them—I was a soft touch.

Being the stepparent and becoming an authority figure over Harvey's children was a challenge, too, because during our first year of marriage, they lived with their mother. When they came to our home on visitation, the girls refused to acknowledge my parental authority. To do so, they felt, would be a betrayal of their mother.

They balked at my authority like I had balked at my brother's. My stepdaughters may not have spoken the words "I don't have to do what you say 'cause you're not the boss of me!" but their attitudes shouted them.

Harvey and I began to recognize patterns of behavior emerging whenever the question of authority was brought up. We could see that neither Harvey nor I could jump right into a place of authority because our children were incapable of making the instant adjustment, and it was unreasonable of us to expect it. Secondly, our children always respected their biological parent's word of authority over the stepparent's. With these observations in mind, we developed a set of simple rules to follow whenever we had to exercise authority over the children.

Eight Simple Rules for Establishing Order of Authority

1. *Talk it through.* Husband and wife communication is extremely important, especially when authority issues are at the center of a conflict. Verbalize your perspectives on the issue at hand.

2. *Apply the "closed door" rule.* Keep disagreements and discussions about your children behind closed doors.

3. *Be in agreement.* Be sure both husband and wife understand the final decision. Do not allow unanswered questions or misunderstandings to surface later. This is the hardest part. If, after all is said and done, the husband and wife still disagree, the wife is obligated to submit to her husband according to God's design.

4. *Pray together.* Praying brings both husband and wife into a place of submission before God. Hard feelings can't remain long if we lay them at the cross.

5. *Listen to your child.* At a separate time when only you (the biological parent), and your child are present, allow your child to express himself. Your child needs to know you are not lost to them as a parent.

6. *Exercise authority in love.* Whenever the final decision is made, do not go behind your spouse's back and tell the child the decision wasn't your (the biological parent) idea. Your child will never accept the stepparent's authority if you do this. The final word, decision, discipline, or reward should be brought to the child by their own parent in love. A child is more likely to accept the final outcome of a situation if it comes from their own parent, rather than from their stepparent.

7. *Be consistent.* Set your boundaries and enforce them. Make sure your child understands both the rules and the consequences up front. When there is an infraction of the rules, the child won't think you're picking on them.

8. *Give it time.* Allow stepparent and stepchild a reasonable measure of time to accept each other. Don't expect instant fixes or immediate bonding. As time goes on and your child trusts the stepparent more, he or she will be able to accept the stepparent's discipline and authority as well.

By keeping to these rules, both sets of children have come to accept and respect both my and Harvey's parental authority. Acceptance and respect did not come overnight, but it happened gradually as we dealt with every child and situation with consistency and love. Some of our kids accepted the situation rather quickly, but for others it took years. I truly believe we have a close family today because Harvey and I were always in unity when we approached the children. Seeing our love and respect for each other made it easier for our children to love and respect their stepparent.

The key to following God's design and keeping his order of authority hinges upon our relationship with him. If we surrender to Christ, surrendering to our spouse is much easier. When I was up against a wall in disagreement with Harvey over some parental issue, I found myself submitting to Christ and his authority over me. It was easier to say yes to God than to Harvey. Ultimately, I was submitting to Harvey out of obedience to Christ. Harvey, too, found it easier to hear my counsel as his helper and wife when he submitted himself to obey Christ.

My husband is my champion—my knight in shining armor. Still, during the difficult years of blending, his armor had to endure a few dings and dents from the punches I threw in my tantrums. My poor husband felt pressure every day—from me, from our kids, and from the exes.

Getting angry and fighting back every time his character was assaulted or his authority was challenged would have been the easy and natural response. He could have given up and thrown in the towel when I cried and complained, but he didn't. Easy as it would have been for Harvey to withdraw from his position as head of the house and just let me handle the kids, he stood firm in his resolve to be the best father and husband that he could be, despite my pity parties and tantrums. His tight hugs were a stabilizing element for both me and our children.

Both parents are essential to tying the family knot securely, but because the husband is the head of your household, he must keep everyone walking on the same path and in the same direction. If the husband has his wife's support, in due season they will reap a harvest from the good seed sown together into their family—this is the divine design.

After their sin was revealed, Adam and Eve pointed fingers of blame away from themselves, but both were guilty. Adam failed in his responsibility as a husband, protector, and head over his wife, Eve. She failed in her responsibility as a wife to bring the decision to her husband and submit to his authority. After Adam and Eve sinned, Adam was cursed: "Because you have listened to the voice of your wife, and have eaten from the tree about which I commanded you, saying, 'You shall not eat from it.' . . ." (Gen. 3:17). When God confronted the two with their sin, neither was willing to accept responsibility for their actions, leaving Satan the victor in that particular battle.

Adam and Eve's failure to accept responsibility went beyond the simple act of eating forbidden fruit. Their ultimate sin was putting their own will and desire above God's, stepping out of his order of authority and its protective covering. I don't know about you, but I don't want Satan to win any more battles in my home. Jesus gave us victory at the cross. We can't have it both ways. We either honor God in obedience to his design and order of authority, or we do things our own way. The choice is ours, but it is our children who will reap what we sow.

A house, or family, is only as stable as the foundation on which it is built. Husbands and wives must accept God's design and be responsible to fulfill their position of authority. So, back to my original question: Who's the boss? Answer: God is the boss when both husband and wife follow his design and order of authority for their home. It is a choice.

Chapter Eight

OH BROTHER!
STEPSIBLING RIVALRY

But he answered and said to his father,
". . . you have never given me a young goat,
so that I might celebrate with my friends."
~ Luke 15:29

Recently, my stepdaughter Sara and I were talking on the phone. In our conversation, she revealed a secret she had kept tucked away in her heart for years. It had to do with an incident that happened years ago on our very first family vacation. When we picked the girls up after their summer visitation with their mom, the van was already loaded down with suitcases and the rest of the family. Instead of going home, we surprised them by heading straight out of town toward Dallas for an extended weekend at Six Flags.

The kids played road games and sang songs along the five-hour drive. At one point, Jennifer and Sara broke out into a cheerful duet. Harvey, who was driving, exclaimed, "My daughters can really sing!" He then turned around and looked at Jennifer to see what her reaction would be because he had never before referred to her as "daughter."

Sara, the other voice in the duet, thought he said, "My daughter can really sing." She didn't hear the *s* on *daughters*. The rejection and jealousy she felt when Harvey turned and looked at Jennifer plagued her for several years. She thought her daddy approved of her stepsister, Jennifer, more than her, his own daughter. When I asked Harvey about this, he said when he turned around, he remembered that Sara looked as if she was mad, but he couldn't figure out why. No one was aware of Sara's feelings.

In my conversation with Sara, she related to me how for years, all the way into high school, she would sing in front of her dad, hoping he would complement her like he did Jennifer that day in the van. When he didn't, the old wound of rejection was torn open again.

CHANGING PLACES

Children in a blended family must often make serious adjustments to their stepsisters and stepbrothers. Like the game musical chairs, everyone has to move into a new slot in the family. In our family alone, all but one of our six kids were thrown into a brand-new position.

My daughter, Jennifer, had always been the only girl; now, all of a sudden, she had three sisters to contend with. Aaron, who was the baby of the family, overnight became big brother to three young girls. Mandi had always been the oldest child, mothering her little sisters. She became the middle child and a little sister herself. Sara, who had been the middle daughter, was now one of the babies of the family. Jodie, the baby of Harvey's family and used to getting everyone's attention, remained the youngest but constantly felt that she had to fight for attention in this new large family. My oldest son, Jeremy, who moved out on his own soon after my marriage to Harvey, was the only one who wasn't affected by our blending.

Along with these new positions came new roles to play. Their pattern of behavior changed just as their responsibilities and sense of self changed. Dr. Kevin Lehman, author of *Living in a Stepfamily without Getting Stepped On,* is an expert on how birth order determines personality, occupational choice, whom you marry, and how you interact with others. He states that in blended families, "unless children are very young, their birth orders don't change, they collide."[1] Instead of everyone fitting into new slots, you now have two sets of birth-order personalities clashing with each other for the same role: two sets of firstborns, two sets of middle children, and two "babies."

While at first the children might feel happy and even excited about gaining new brothers or sisters, they often feel jealous and betrayed as they watch their own mom or dad take on the parenting role with their new siblings.

STEPSIBLING ISSUES

Counting the conflicts between the kids throughout our years of blending would be as difficult as counting the stars. Most fights were your everyday brother/sister or sister/sister arguments. Although the actual stepsibling conflicts may have been fewer in number, they were considerably deeper in ramification. Blended families are as diverse as fingerprints, while the combinations can be as limitless as the obstacles they must overcome. Simple issues that are easily resolved in a nuclear family can become deep wounds in the blended family if no one recognizes or deals with them.

I have found that stepsibling issues usually fall into at least one of three categories: jealousy, resentfulness, or rejection. Children can experience jealousy for their parent's attention, feel resentfulness over losing their place in the family, or imagine rejection when their parent embraces the new family members. Not all, but many of these stepsibling issues stem from a child's feelings of insecurity in their parent's love.

You can see these issues of insecurity as little seedlings, popping up in eruptions of anger over simple complements, a gift, an item in the closet, or a sandwich taken off the counter. These actions can be translated as: "You don't care about me anymore," "He's trying to take my place," or "I'm not important."

Depending on how far along you are in your blending process, you can either prevent these seeds from taking root, nip them in the bud, or weed them out by working together with your child on a one-on-one basis—one weed at a time. You can recognize the kind of weed and how far along it has grown by putting yourself into your child's world—seeing things through his or her eyes.

A Child's World

A child's world, even a teenager's, is small and contained within their own realm of experience. They cannot see beyond what they've experienced. Because they are children, their world revolves around them. They aren't being selfish—it is just all they know. It takes a clear explanation or a tangible demonstration to bring the bigger picture, abstract ideas, and concepts down into a child's world and understanding. Actually, this is the natural condition of human beings in general—we must be *taught* to see beyond ourselves.

For instance, at our youngest daughter's wedding, my grandson Stephen was chosen as the ring bearer. Stephen is a normal eight-year-old boy who has trouble standing still for more than a minute.

During the rehearsal for the wedding, he continually flipped the ring bearer pillow, fidgeted, and looked around the whole time while he was standing on the platform. It was very distracting, and we were all concerned that he would do this during the wedding. So after the rehearsal, when it was just the two of us, I had a talk with him.

In our talk, we discussed the wedding ceremony and what it was all about. I told him how his Aunt Jodie and her fiancé were promising to love each other and be with each other for the rest of their lives. They were making their promise in front of God, and all the people were coming to the church to hear them do this. I then explained to him that because this was a very important time for his aunt, everyone would be quiet, watching and listening to her and the groom. After setting the picture in young Stephen's mind, I told him that if the people up on the platform were goofing off, looking around, or fidgeting, everyone would be looking at them instead of the bride and groom. The important promises would be missed, and that is why he had to stand very still and not fidget with the pillow. After Stephen asked a few questions, such as "Why am I carrying fake rings on a pillow?" and "How many people will be there to hear Aunt Jodie make the promise?" he seemed satisfied and at ease about the whole wedding thing.

The next day, at the actual wedding, Stephen walked down the aisle like a young man. He stood in his place on the platform, never moving. The expression on his face was solemn and attentive. The flower girl, on the other hand, had no such "wedding talk" in her realm of experience. She dumped the flower basket and fidgeted the whole time.

Unlike Stephen, the flower girl did not understand the significance of the moment. Both children were the same age. The only difference was their understanding of the event. The "wedding talk" expanded Stephen's world to include the importance of his part in the wedding.

We can expand our child's world in the blended family by giving them a tangible understanding of their importance and reaffirming our love for them. For example, when a stepchild blows up about a little thing, talk to her about the bigger world and, perhaps more importantly, be prepared to listen to her questions. Tune in to your child's level of understanding and help them see the bigger picture: they are not the center of the universe. Don't just tell them, "Stop it, that's bad!" Explain why their behavior is inappropriate—why one sister gets to do this, but the other can't. Sally can't eat all of the cookies because Billy wants one too.

An Adult's World

While a child sees only his immediate world, an adult is looking at the big picture. When we remarry and become a blended family, our world of thinking is usually inclusive of mom, dad, and all the kids. We look at every member of the family and work at bringing them together, but it is easy to overlook our children's need for personal attention from their biological parent. Remarriage after divorce or the death of a parent has a way of shaking the stable ground our kids walk on.

Sara's story is a good example of how differently children and adults think. Harvey, the adult, was looking at the big picture—bringing his family together. He was aware of Jennifer and her envy of his daughters' relationship with him because she and her father were never close. She saw how he loved them, laughed and joked with them, and made them feel special. She always felt like an outsider. Harvey was attempting to make Jennifer feel as though she had a dad.

A parent's world must include every child while performing a delicate balancing act of love and attention between them. We need to be aware and try to meet each child's need without neglecting the others. If we lean too much one way or the other, we're likely to face a fall. Harvey made the mistake of assuming Sara was secure in his love.

In Luke 15, Jesus tells a story about a father and his two sons. Though we commonly refer to this parable as the prodigal son, I want to focus on the older brother. Big brother stayed at home with his father, working hard and doing everything he was told, while the younger brother cashed in his inheritance and went on a partying spree. Although Jesus didn't portray them as stepsiblings, the same jealousies existed.

After blowing all of his inheritance, the younger brother realized the error of his ways and returned home to his father. Dad saw him coming up the road and ran to greet him, welcoming him back with a kiss and a celebration. The older son's insecurity with his father made his younger brother appear as a threat. Thinking as a child, the older son exploded in anger, resentment, and jealousy when he saw his father embrace and welcome the younger son back into the family.

From the older son's perspective, his father was being unfair. The son felt betrayed because, after all, he had always been a good son and had more of a right to a party. His younger brother had taken advantage of his dad, and now, here he was, back home living it up—with his dad's blessing.

The older brother immediately pointed out to his father all of his own good behavior and how he had been a model son. He also expressed his jealousy when he said, "You have never given *me* a young goat, so that I might celebrate with *my* friends!" (Luke 15:29, italics added). This short statement sums up the jealousy and outrage the older son felt for his little brother. Like Sara, he was looking for his father's approval through performance.

Sara, who was about eight years old at the time of our first vacation, could only see Jennifer, her brothers, and me as a threat. The divorce of her parents was especially difficult for her. Her ground was shaken because she felt that my children and I were taking her daddy away. Harvey had always been a doting father, but it didn't sit well with Sara when he displayed the same kind of fatherly love toward her stepsiblings. Sara felt the same outrage and betrayal the older son felt in Jesus' parable.

As parents, we need to recognize our children's way of thinking. They want and need our approval, but it's up to us to show them that our love isn't based on performance. The father in Jesus' parable pointed out to the older brother something he couldn't see for himself. The father had no need to give him a party and kill the fattened calf because all the calves already belonged to his son, and he could take as many as he liked, as often as he liked. The father reassured his older son of his unlimited love for him by saying, "You have always been with me" (Luke 15:31). His love wasn't based on what the son did or how well he performed; he loved him simply because he was his son.

When the father saw his son's resentfulness and jealousy over the attention the returning prodigal was being given, *the father immediately went to him* (see Luke 15:28). He assured the son of his love and explained the importance of accepting the younger brother.

Harvey was feeling the same fatherly love toward Sara. She had always been with him and always had his love. Everything he had already belonged to her because she was his daughter.

I'm certain that if Harvey had realized at the time how deeply his comment affected Sara, he also would have gone to her and talked about it. The problem is, we don't always know when our children are hurting. They don't always tell us. Sometimes, like Sara, they carry it around with them for years.

COMMUNICATING LOVE

Because our children don't always communicate with us, especially when they feel threatened, we must consistently affirm and communicate our love to them. It may not seem like anything is bothering them, and maybe nothing is, but an extra hug or a little one-on-one time speaks volumes in the language of love.

We can prevent those early seeds of jealousy from taking root by tangibly expressing love to our children. The best way to do this is by spending time with them. Don't make the mistake of thinking everything must be done as a "family." Our children need to be reassured that they haven't lost their mom or dad. Set aside one-on-one time with each of your biological kids, apart from your spouse and their children.

If you used to play catch with your son before you remarried, continue to have that time with him. Go ahead and have a family ball team that includes everyone, just keep your time with your son intact. If you have a teenage daughter, spend some special time with her. Go to the mall, get a manicure together, or bake some cookies—anything that communicates, "I'm still your mom and I love you." If you affirm or complement one child, Harvey will tell you to make sure you purposefully do the same with the other children as well.

Talk to your kids on their level. They need you. My daughter longed for time alone with mom. She was a teenage girl who needed to talk once in a while—not necessarily about any big, important issue—just mother-daughter time. She didn't want to have her little stepsisters in on everything we did. Sometimes she just needed me.

Likewise, Harvey's daughters needed time alone with their dad—without me and my kids. Our kids need to know their parent isn't lost to them just because he or she got married. When we try to force our blending by insisting that everyone do everything together, resentments result.

STEPSIBLING SCENARIOS

Sometimes the logistics of a household are such that bathrooms and bedrooms must be shared. This is a hard adjustment for some children, especially teens, but if our kids feel secure in their parent's love, they'll come through it. We can open a line of communication with our child by being a compassionate ear to our child's complaints. Lecturing them on sharing or telling them how tight money is only magnifies the reality of the big change in our child's life. Yes, they may have to share, but if we've been a listening ear, they'll know we see them and care—this is huge to a child.

Let's go into our child's world. Here are some scenarios to consider. Maybe you'll see your children in one of these situations:

- Your daughter has always been an only child. Think about how hard it is for her suddenly to share a bathroom with two brothers.

- You are a father with two teenage daughters who live with their mother. You've remarried, and your wife's kids are now sleeping in your daughters' old rooms. Now your daughters don't want to visit anymore.

- Your stepson was used to playing catch with his dad on the weekends. Consider how he would feel if his special time were changed from "catch with dad" to playing ball with a whole team of girls.

- Your son is just learning to play ball. *Catching* the ball was a big deal before, but now his new stepbrother, the star player on an older league, has joined in the game. Simply catching the ball doesn't seem to mean so much to you anymore. Now that everyone is always talking about what a great player his stepbrother is, your son doesn't want to play at all.

These scenarios and countless others describe the frustration and insecurity a child feels when their world is disrupted by their parent's remarriage. They've already been through one huge transition when their parents divorced or they lost a parent through death. Making adjustments to a whole new family doesn't come easily for most kids. The insecurities they feel make them cling even more to their mom or dad—the one stabilizing factor in their world. Their clinging comes out in resentments and jealousies toward their new stepsiblings. Silly things, such as singing in the backseat, become huge issues of rejection.

In the blending process we, as adults, should consider the limited world in which our children live. By talking with them and affirming them in our love, we open up their understanding and their vision. We don't have to get deep and philosophical with young kids—just be real. Believe me, children grab a lot more than we give them credit for. But when we don't take the time to talk with our kids or affirm them, a situation like Sara's can easily develop. Had Harvey realized the wound created in Sara's young heart that day, he would have prevented it by complementing her socks off. She's a great singer!

Stepsibling rivalry can be a real headache for parents to deal with. But if we parents can put ourselves into our children's world and see things through their eyes for just a little while, we can love them through anything. The good news is that our kids grow up; and as our children grow up into adulthood, so does their world of thinking. If we have been consistent in affirming our children, they will grow past the need to cling to us in jealousy or in desperation. A transformation in their thinking process makes them see their stepsiblings in a different light as well. Sara now thinks of Jennifer as her sister, not Terri's daughter. She is no longer threatened by Jennifer as she was when she was eight. It's amazing the difference a little consistent love and a few years can make. Sara now feels confident in her relationship with her daddy. She feels secure in his love—and it's OK that he loves Jennifer too.

Chapter Nine

THE PERPLEXES OF THE EXES

Love . . . is not provoked, does not
take into account a wrong suffered.
~ 1 Corinthians 13:4–5

The first thought that comes to mind as I begin this chapter is *tread lightly*. Like tiptoeing through a field of land mines, one misplaced step can have disastrous results. The ex is a touchy topic because we are cracking open the door of the past just enough to allow those old feelings of anger, mistrust, betrayal, and pain to be exposed. Yes, God has blessed us with a wonderful new relationship, and we have remarried, expecting to turn that page in our lives and begin a fresh new chapter. Tender wounds from our past, however, often exist just below the surface after divorce. These wounds affect how we approach the ex-wife or husband, and believe me, our children, with wounds of their own, watch, hear, and feel how we behave toward their mom or dad. Remember, we are training them up in the way they should go (see Prov. 22:6). The old saying "Do as I say, not as I do" doesn't work here. Our responsibility is to "walk our talk."

To many divorcees, just the thought of dealing with the ex is perplexing, to say the least. Thoughts of past conflicts with their ex bring on cold sweats, high blood pressure, and the heebie-jeebies. Be that as it may, the former spouse is still very much a part of the blended family equation—they are our children's other parent. Our children are not divorced from their other parent; in fact, that parent is usually still an important part of their lives. All too often, however, even in a Christian home, the divorced parents continue to approach each other with resentments and anger. Consequently, the children get caught in the middle between their mom and dad—two people they love. The parents must set the example in the home. If we want our children to honor and respect us, we have to set an example by honoring and respecting their other parent. This includes being civil toward them, both when the children are around and when they are not. This means, "Doing what's right when nobody's looking."

PUTTING AWAY THE CHILD

Sometimes I really miss being a kid. When I was a kid, it was up to the grown-ups to make all of the decisions and plans. The responsibility of doing the right thing for the family was on their shoulders, not mine. I was just a kid. My biggest problems were in my homework assignments. But, let's face it, we all have to grow up sometime.

As much as we hate to admit it, *we* are the grown-ups in our families, and *we* need to put away our childishness. Paul put it best in 1 Corinthians 13:11, writing: "When I was a child, I used to speak like a child, think like a child, reason like a child; when I became a man, I did away with childish things." As children, we do a lot of silly, childish things.

When I was a young girl, we lived in an incredible two-story house with a basement. The best thing about this house was the laundry chute. Looking back, I can remember two of my -brothers and me thinking of the fun we would have dropping our youngest brother down the chute from the second floor all the way into the big laundry bin in the basement. We prepared a soft landing by piling a bunch of dirty clothes into the bin. After some discussion and protests from our brother about whether he should go in head first or feet first, we put little Art into the chute with his feet leading (although if he had a choice, I'm sure his feet would have run the other way). With all the excitement and anticipation one would expect at a NASA space mission, we took our positions. My oldest brother was on the second floor holding Art at the opening, ready to launch. My other brother was at the chute door on the first floor to watch him go by, while I was at the laundry bin in the basement for the catch. Our excitement quickly turned into disappointment, though, because our poor little brother got stuck a few feet into his ride. We considered slicking him down with some smelly stuff from one of the jars on mom's dresser, but my brothers didn't want to smell like girls. Our childish reasoning only resulted in a bruised up little brother who proved to be too big for the chute, no matter how hard we tried to shove or stuff him.

As part of growing up, I have had to put childish thinking behind me. Now, thinking as an adult, I would never attempt to put my little brother down that chute. One look and I could easily size up the whole situation—my little brother is still much bigger than the laundry chute. Don't laugh because many of us think as an adult but still reason as a child, oblivious to the pending disaster that can result. Children don't look at the big picture to see the consequences of their actions; they live for the moment. Thinking as an adult, one could easily see the physical dilemma; but more than that, an adult also reasons, "The poor kid could have been hurt going down that chute!"

Do you remember Baby Jessica? The whole country watched the real-life drama being played out on the television news. Little Baby Jessica had fallen into a well and was stuck too far down for anyone to reach her. For days the two-year-old's mother sang nursery rhymes to her while crews of skilled men and women with special equipment dug another hole beside the one Jessica was in. When they finally pulled her out safely, you could hear the cheers across America. What if my little brother had made it halfway between the floors and we couldn't reach him? Our childish reasoning could have resulted in my brother making the headlines.

Maybe you can identify with this example of thinking as an adult but reasoning as a child. In my years of blending, packing bags for visitation was a biweekly ritual. I would send nice clothes many times, but only *some* of them would return. Over and over again, I would remind the girls to please be sure to bring everything home. After the weekend visitation was over, we would get ready for school on Monday, and guess what? No jeans. Two weeks would pass before the girls could retrieve the needed clothes at their mother's home. After months of missing everything from socks, underwear, jeans, and shirts to coats and homework assignments, I made up my mind that I would pack only old clothes that I didn't care about getting back. Oblivious to the problems this would cause, I stuffed those old clothes into a bag the same way I tried to stuff my little brother down the chute.

Whatever the reason for the clothes being overlooked, whether they were left in the laundry, kicked under a bed, or eaten by Peewee the dog, I was fed up. I harbored resentments toward my husband's ex-wife for "keeping" the clothes and not being responsible enough to send them back. In my mind, I felt my solution was justified. I told myself I was thinking only of the girls; they needed their good clothes for school.

As a result of *my* childish reasoning, while at their mother's house they had to wear clothes all weekend long that they didn't like, were stained, or didn't fit well. For playing outside, this was fine; however, if they went anywhere special, all they had to wear were old clothes. This made the girls unhappy and gave them reason to resent me. Not only did the girls resent me, but the hot coals in our relationship with my husband's ex-wife were fanned into flames. Things were sizzling hot around the Clark house.

All of this could have been avoided had I put away my childish reasoning. I allowed my mind to make the situation worse than it had to be. It was hard for me, in my frustration over this "missing clothes" situation, to see past my husband's ex-wife to the big picture—or the consequences of my stubbornness. Thankfully, God, in his mercy, tapped me on the shoulder with a few words of wisdom. I read in 2 Corinthians 10:3–4: "Though we walk in the flesh, we do not war according to the flesh, for the weapons of our warfare are not of the flesh, but divinely powerful for the destruction of fortresses." God was showing me that I had some serious fortresses built up in my mind against Harvey's ex-wife, and I was warring against her in my flesh.

God reminded me that Satan was out to destroy my family, and I was buying right into his plan with my "fleshy" responses. Satan was the real enemy, not the ex-wife. The next verse (2 Cor. 10:5) talks about taking our thoughts captive to the obedience of Christ. That got my attention! I finally recognized that I was actually being disobedient to Christ with my childish reasoning and actions. God was instructing me to take those thoughts captive so they wouldn't be free to do any more damage. I had to regain the vision of a solid home being built upon the Rock.

Our thoughts are where many a battle can be won or lost. If we don't gain control of our thoughts, we will surely lose the war. God gives us the weapons to pull down the fortresses we build in our minds (see 2 Cor. 10:4). These aren't weapons we can see or touch, but they are "divinely powerful." When encountering emotional situations with your or your spouse's ex, the first thing you have to do is recognize with whom you are doing battle. Your enemy, as well as the battlefield, is spiritual, not physical.

Knowing Satan's schemes is like the president of the United States knowing the exact plan of a future terrorist attack. A good leader doesn't sit around waiting for the hit; he assembles the men and means to crush the enemy in his tracks *before* he can do any damage. In the same way, God expects us to put away our childishness, using wisdom to reason as adults. Encouragement comes from Romans 16:19–20: "I want you to be wise in what is good and innocent in what is evil. The God of peace will soon crush Satan under your feet." Because we act on what we know, we'll be dancing over a crushed and defeated enemy.

In my weekend, bag-stuffing situation, I had to change my strategy by forgiving the girls and their mother. The first step was taking a hard look at the actual problem, as well as the *real* enemy— minus the thought-exaggerated blame game. The problem was in the children being children. In their last-minute haste to repack their bags before coming home, they missed or forgot things. I knew the girls were responsible for gathering up their own things, and this was something I had no control over.

The solution was to make a list for each child of every-thing that was packed into their bag, with short descriptions if necessary. They could go down the list, item by item, as they repacked their bags. If they didn't bring something back, they had to suffer the consequences. Doing without a coat, redoing homework, or living without their jeans or favorite clothes for two weeks was the consequence for their own neglect or forgetfulness. Harvey's ex-wife was removed from the battlefield, and I no longer had reason to resent her for not returning the clothes with the girls. Suitcase closed.

A Case for Love

Paul talked about putting away childish things in the context of love. His description of love isn't all mushy and dripping with sentiment; on the contrary, it is challenging to one's faith. He talked about loving in a way that goes against our nature—especially when we are wronged! Take a look at this passage in 1 Corinthians 13, keeping your exes in mind.

> Love is patient, love is kind and is not jealous; love does not brag and is not arrogant, does not act unbecomingly; it does not seek its own, is not provoked, does not take into account a wrong suffered, does not rejoice in unrighteousness, but rejoices with the truth; bears all things, believes all things, hopes all things, endures all things. (1 Cor. 13:4–7)

Now look at it again, resisting the temptation of thinking you need to send this Scripture anonymously in a letter to your ex so they will treat you better. It is written to you and to me. This is a description of how Christians are to behave toward other people—even those who are disrespectful, mean, and downright ugly toward us.

The responsibility of teaching our children moral integrity and respect falls squarely on us because we are the parents *and* we are Christians. Difficult as it might be, we must look past any grievances we might have with our ex-spouse and demonstrate, by our behavior toward them, the love Paul wrote about in 1 Corinthians 13. Talk about tough love!

The commandment handed down to us by Moses, right behind honoring God and putting him first in our lives, is "Honor your father and your mother" (Deut. 5:16). This is a commandment, not a request. No problem; I honor my parents. I have no problem with my children honoring their other parent either; but when *I* don't honor their other parent, I am nullifying the Word of God for my kids. The other parent doesn't have to be nice, reasonable, or respectful toward us for this commandment to apply. In fact, in many cases, just the opposite is true.

Our children need for us to behave respectfully toward their other mom or dad. If you are willing to honor a person out of respect for God, you can be assured that God will return honor to you. That doesn't mean you have to bake them cookies or buy them a Christmas gift; it just means that as far as it is up to you, be peaceable (Rom. 12:18). The -million-dollar question here is, How do you practice love toward someone you dislike and who may dislike you? This is a question that has plagued Christians for centuries. The answer is, *you* can't. Neither could I. But *in Christ* we can do all things (see Phil. 4:13).

Listen to the thing Paul had to live with: "There was given me a thorn in the flesh, a messenger of Satan to torment me—to keep me from exalting myself! Concerning this I implored the Lord three times that it might leave me. And He [Jesus] has said to me, 'My grace is sufficient for you, for power is perfected in weakness'" (2 Cor. 12:7–9).

Does your thorn bear any resemblance to Paul's? Have you asked God to remove it from your life? The Lord's answer to Paul's request for its removal was *no*. Why? The Lord said that his grace was enough to enable Paul to live with his thorn. In fact, the Lord even indicated that it was through Paul's weakness and inability to remove it, forcing him to *live with it,* that he would gain power over it. When encountering an obnoxious, irrational, or abusive ex-husband or wife, our weakness is the very means by which God can show himself strong on our behalf. Like a hand in a glove, it is God working through our willingness to be obedient to his will in our lives. A glove takes on the shape and strength of the hand; but without the actual hand fitted inside, it can do nothing. When we rely upon God, his strength and wisdom become our own, enabling us to live with our thorn.

Did you notice where God placed the emphasis in Paul's thorny problem? God wanted to strengthen Paul and keep him from pride and vanity—the same things that led to the fall of Satan and man. The thorn actually had purpose—to keep Paul from exalting himself. Look at your thorn in the same light. God wants to strengthen you, to give you the ability to walk through this situation and keep you from exalting yourself with pride by redirecting your focus. Read 1 Corinthians 13 one more time. It says that love is not arrogant, does not act unbecomingly; it does not seek its own, is not provoked, and does not take into account a wrong suffered. These attitudes can only happen when our focus is on God rather than ourselves.

So how do you practice love toward someone you dislike and who may dislike you? If your ex is prone to dramatic Jerry-Springer-type scenes or is abusive or impossible to work with, allow the strength of God's hand to move in your glove. Bite your tongue, take your eyes off yourself, and focus your eyes on the road in front of you, relying on the power of God to get you there.

Taking the High Road

For years Harvey and I had to drive to Little Rock from our home in Pearcy every other weekend to pick up or drop off the girls for visitation with their mother. We were just one of several minivans that made the biweekly exchange in the McDonald's parking lot.

While waiting, my husband and I used to make a game of analyzing all of the exchange families. We would try to match them up and then decide which ones got along and which ones couldn't wait to get out of there. We would all show up about the same time, around five o'clock, on Friday or Sunday evening to pick up or drop off our kids. One by one, moms or dads would show up, give their final hugs and kisses, transfer the bags, close the doors, fasten the seat belts, and drive off in opposite directions—that is, everyone but us. We were still sitting there, waiting—sometimes waiting as much as an hour past the specified time—always the first ones to arrive and the last ones to leave.

The scenario went something like this: At 5:00 we would be sitting in the van, listening to all the chatter over school, activities, friends, and anything else little girls like to talk about. As time passes, the girls grow restless and begin to get hungry. We agree to go through the drive-through at McDonald's and feed everyone at about 5:15. By 5:30 we are scanning every car that turns the corner for any sign of Harvey's ex-wife's vehicle. The tension in the van grows as I take on an attitude of resentment. We aren't saying anything, but Harvey and I are both feeling it. *Ticktock, ticktock.* I keep looking at the clock, knowing that with each minute that passes, the likelihood of dinner and a movie becomes slim to none. Somewhere around 5:45 or 6:00 the car pulls up and the exchange is made. Too late to manage both dinner and a movie, we go to a nice restaurant to eat before driving back home.

I'd like to say that I would then enjoy the rest of the evening with my husband and make the best of the situation, but that would be pure fabrication. The truth is, I usually pouted and felt sorry for myself. I resented the intrusion on our date, and I hated always having to go the extra mile; but we were resolved never to take issue with her if we could avoid it, especially in front of the children. In other words, we took the high road.

There are two ways for us to get home from Little Rock—Highway 70 West or Interstate 30 to Highway 270W. Both routes end up in Hot Springs, just a stone's throw from our home in Pearcy. The difference between the two highways is the mountains: one road goes over them while the other avoids them. Harvey and I always take the high road over the mountains on Highway 70. Although this is a two-lane road for the most part, there are certain places where you can pass slower vehicles. The two benefits to taking this route are the scenery and time; it is a beautiful drive and a more direct route than the other road.

Taking the high road in life's situations requires us to travel over the mountains and the rough places, sometimes getting behind someone who slows us down. If we keep our eyes on the Lord, even though that person holding us up may be irritating, we will get past them eventually. God knows how we feel when we encounter those hard-to-manage people, but he also gives us what we need to keep going. Our children are paying attention to their scenery. If we want them to grow up in the secure environment of our love, we must take the high road by controlling our tempers and avoiding as many conflicts with their other parent as possible. The road may be more difficult, but it will get us where we want to go much quicker than the alternative.

THE MISSING PARENT

Up to this point, I have been talking about the perplexes of the exes you have to deal with on a regular basis. Life would be so much easier for us if we could have only one set of kinks to work through in our family knot-tying process. Life, however, is usually pretty good about weaving several colors of thread with varying textures into our tapestry.

Some of the threads in our tapestry are invisible, like clear fishing line. Holding and weaving something you can't see is a difficult process. Fishing line only looks invisible, but don't be fooled into thinking it doesn't exist, or you'll wind up like the fish at the end of the hook.

My ex-husband seldom interfered with the rearing of our children because he was never around. For me, as an ex-wife, this was fine; but for my children, this invisible thread left a hole in the overall design of the tapestry. This part of our family knot was especially difficult for us to tie.

The silence of a parent's absence in a child's life sometimes rings louder than the clanging of a parent who is always there. For many children, there is just enough presence to disappoint. Their parent promises to pick the child up for a visit and then doesn't show. The child sits at the window, bags packed, waiting one eternal hour after another until bedtime finally brings their wait to a heartbreaking close. Scenarios of similar disparagement can be seen at ball games, school plays, band recitals, and birthday parties where children expectantly wait for a dad or mom who promised to come but doesn't. The instinctive reaction to this kind of treatment is similar to a mother bear protecting her cub. Watch out for the claws! Justified as it may seem, God really does have a better way for us and for our children.

Keep in mind the reason for your child's disappointment; they love their parent, they want to be with them, and they are holding onto the hope of returned love. Verbally tearing up their dad or mom only adds to a child's insecurity. It may make you feel better; however, the child no longer feels they can trust you with their feelings because of your negative response toward someone they are struggling to hang on to. At this time of disappointment and pain, bear hugs are a more desirable alternative to bear claws.

I thought it would be easy for Harvey, as a stepfather, to step right in and assume the dad role left by my children's absent father. However, broken promises, forgotten birthdays, and unacknowledged holidays bore holes of insecurity and feelings of rejection in my children. The guarded wall around their hearts was so securely built that accepting a "new dad" was especially difficult for them. The children wanted their father's attention, and whenever Harvey did the "dad things" with them or for them, it just magnified the hole left by their father's absence.

Like a mother bird with her protective wing, I found myself playing guard over my kids when Harvey wanted to discipline them or even address an issue. I wanted to know what the problem was, what he was going to say to them, and exactly why he thought they needed to be disciplined. These were all legitimate questions, but the anxiety I felt wasn't. More often than not, I tried to protect my children from Harvey's discipline.

I'm thankful now that we implemented the closed-door rule early in our marriage, because if my kids heard all of my questioning, they never would have respected Harvey or his judgments. Because I knew my children's hearts were already wounded, I wanted to be sure they wouldn't have to deal with more rejection. God showed me that I had to trust Harvey. He was my husband, and that made him *my* covering. When he covered me, he also covered my children.

One of my sons recently told me that the unity Harvey and I demonstrated in our home has meant more to him than anything else, growing up in a blended family. At the time he didn't like his stepdad very much or the decisions he made concerning him. What kid does? But now that he is an adult, he sees how it formed in him a sense of respect for authority and a feeling of security. My husband enjoys the sincere love and respect of all three of my children because of his love, wisdom, and integrity as a father. This love and respect, however, could not have been developed if he were not permitted to discipline or *be* a father to my children.

Everything comes back to our foundation. We said our vows and pledged ourselves to each other with Christ as the foundation of our home. Harvey and I committed to our marriage and worked at talking to each other about all the things we felt concerning our children. Christ, communication, and commitment have carried us through every emotional struggle concerning our children and our exes.

The hardest thing for parents to do who live in the same house with all of the children day by day is to sort through emotions over how the other biological parents, as well as our spouse, are treating our kids. We see how an ex's interference, as well as their absence, affects our children. Never was there a more appropriate saying than "You can mess with me, but don't mess with my kids." We want our children to grow up happy and emotionally healthy, protecting them at all costs—even the cost of our marriage. Is it any wonder there are so many divorces in second marriages with children? Our three elements of Christ, commitment, and communication are critical to our marriage and family stability.

Anyone who has been through divorce with children probably has a list of offenses to overcome. You can probably tell your own stories of what you have had to live with on a day-to-day basis concerning your ex. The important thing to remember though is to think and reason as an adult by putting away childish things.

My little brother was relieved when our plan to drop him down the chute failed. He, like our children, was the victim of childish reasoning. Because the ex-spouse is our children's mom or dad, we must take the high road by walking in the tough love Paul described in 1 Corinthians 13. Otherwise, we could end up with bruised children who don't fit into the chute or, worse yet, children caught in the middle of an impossible, downward fall.

Chapter Ten

VISITATION:
THE PERMANENT WAVE

Give Your servant an understanding heart . . .
to discern between good and evil.
~ 1 Kings 3:9

*L*ike the surf of the sea, rolling and breaking in constant motion, so are the emotions of a child during visitation. Saying hello to one parent while waving good-bye to the other brings happiness and sadness crashing head to head. Confusion over these mixed feelings often trigger behavioral changes in our children, such as anger, rebellion, or withdrawal. Corralling all of the conflicting emotions and bringing them under control can be as frustrating as herding kittens.

My daughter's eight-year-old son, Stephen, has two kittens named Laverne and Shirley. They are always romping, scampering, and hiding all over the house. In fact, their favorite game is hide-and-seek. One evening, while playing out the "seeking" role in the kitten's game, Stephen spotted Shirley right away, but Laverne was nowhere to be found. While searching for the elusive kitten, Stephen's mother told him it was time for bed.

Stephen brushed his teeth, said his prayers, and exchanged hugs, kisses, and good-nights with his mom before the lights were turned off. With the covers securely tucked in, he nestled down to sleep. Just as he was drifting off, he was startled by a bump in the night. Stephen climbed out of bed to tell his mother that something was in his room. Searching for the source of the bumping noise, Jennifer checked the closet, under the bed, and each of the dresser drawers, finding nothing. She assured her son that everything was all right, kissed him good-night, and then turned off the light.

Stephen settled down to go to sleep when he heard it again—*Bump!* Running out to his mom, he complained once more about the noise. They both returned to the room, carefully checking the closet, drawers, and under the bed. Rather disquieted, Stephen climbed back under the covers. All of their rummaging had only turned up toys and clothes—but no source of the mysterious noises. Yet no sooner had Jennifer turned out the light and left the room when—*bump, bump, bump*—there it was again! "Mom!" Stephen yelled, "something *really is* in my room!"

By this time Jennifer's patience was growing thin as she told him, "Stephen, I'll check one more time, but there is nothing in your room." No doubt, the skittish eight-year-old had visions of creepy things lurking in the corners and hiding in the dark. Stephen's mom opened the closet door—nothing. She looked under the bed—nothing. She opened the top drawer—nothing. She opened the second drawer, expecting nothing as well, but as soon as it was opened, Laverne made a tremendous leap out and onto the floor.

Stephen screamed, cried, laughed, and hyperventilated all at the same time. He didn't know how to respond to the kitten scurrying across the floor because at the moment of surprise, every possible emotion came rushing up to the surface. He was afraid of the scary goblin jumping out of his drawer, relieved that it was just Laverne, happy that she was found, and tickled that his kitten was so funny. As you can imagine, calming poor little Stephen down for bed required some serious reassurance and very tight hugs from his mother.

Visitation also leaps out at our children. As a result of being split between parents, emotions such as anger, hurt, frustration, or guilt often slip out of our kids without warning. Those feelings can be interpreted as rejection or rebellion. Parents are caught off guard by how visitation affects their kids. Seeing past a child's behavior is difficult, but like Stephen, our kids need some serious reassurance and very tight hugs while they are riding the waves of "visitation."

Because parents also get confused and overwhelmed by these waves, we need our share of tight hugs and reassurance as well. By turning to our Father and seeking his wisdom, we receive an understanding heart. God shows us how consistency and love provide our children with the security they need. As he forms an understanding heart in us, we learn how to let go of the little things, trusting God to bring balance and calm to our homes.

PART-TIME KIDS, FULL-TIME PARENTS

When our kids are on visitation—whether it is for an hour, a weekend, a week, a month, a summer, or a year—we are always mom or dad. Even when our children live with the other parent, our role doesn't change. We are full-time parents, even if our children are only with us part-time. How we bear and express this responsibility significantly affects our children's character development as well as the stability they feel in the home.

Harvey and I found that consistency was extremely important to our family's stability. Because so many parts of our children's lives were moving and shifting, they needed us to be unchanging in order to feel safe. The rules remained the same, day after day. Don't get me wrong—our kids didn't always like our rules or our way of doing things. However, they knew our love was as consistent as the rules.

During the first year of our marriage, Harvey's three daughters lived with their mother while two of my children lived with us. My oldest son was out of school and living on his own. Even though some of our family members were only living with us part-time, we considered everyone as part of our family. We thought of ourselves as permanent parents, running our household as if everyone was living there. We wanted to demonstrate to our children that we were always within reach, even when time spent with us was brief.

In our home there was a bed for each child. We set definite bedtimes for weekdays and weekends, as well as guidelines for permissible music, TV programs, and movies. Homework was done every day after school, and everyone attended church on Sundays and Wednesdays. None of these things changed, whether there were five children present or two. When we received custody of the girls, the rules remained consistent. Our routines changed to accommodate a larger full-time household, but our rules and standards were securely fixed.

Consistency in our household provided a wall of security for all of the children. The wall of security around our kids was built one solid brick at a time and was found to be secure as each of our children's lives shifted from one household to the next. Harvey's oldest daughter, Mandi, transitioned into the middle child of a blended family, but Daddy was still Daddy. Aaron shifted from being the baby of the family to big brother, but Mom was still Mom. Everyone still had to clean their rooms and carry their load.

No one was coddled or favored because of their changing world; they were just securely loved.

Jennifer and Aaron, who were living at home full-time, knew that the rules wouldn't change because their three stepsisters had moved in. Mandi, Sara, and Jodie, who were going through a radical environmental change, knew that they were equal members of their dad's household—under the same rules as those who had been there all along. All of the children knew what to expect from Harvey and me; this part of their lives remained consistent and unmoving.

How would Stephen have felt if his mother had not been there for him to run to when he heard those bumps in the night? He knew he could trust and rely on her, and even though she was losing patience with the whole ordeal, she was the source of his security. His fears could not overtake him as long as Mom was within reach. He knew, without a doubt, that she loved him and wouldn't stop loving him, even if he came running to her over and over again.

Our children also felt safe inside the boundaries we set for them, but this is not to say we didn't have problems. The perfectly blended family is only a television fantasy. I remember watching *The Brady Bunch* on TV, where every family issue and attitude was resolved in a thirty-minute episode. Wouldn't that be nice? Unfortunately, the reality of life is far more complex than that.

When our families move in together, we each bring our baggage with us. Unpacking our rejections, fears, and insecurities is a slow and tedious process. We've been wearing those old clothes for so long, it is hard to part with them, so we tend to stuff them into the drawers and closets of our new home. Parenting is a tough job for any mom or dad, but parenting our kids through visitation and blending presents many unique and unforeseen challenges. Hidden emotional surprises lurk in every drawer and closet of our children's minds—and ours too. Like Stephen's kitten, they jump out when we are least expecting them.

AN UNDERSTANDING HEART

Harvey and I wrote our own marriage vows to each other. I promised to honor Harvey as my husband and love his children as my own. At the time this seemed to be an easy-to-fulfill vow. It didn't take long, however, to discover that this was an enormous responsibility, requiring an understanding heart and God's wisdom. After only a few experiences with visitation, the pressure was on.

In order to make wise decisions in the midst of emotional surprises, we must turn to God. The Bible says, "If any of you lacks wisdom, let him ask of God, who gives to all generously and without reproach, and it will be given to him" (James 1:5). God's wisdom is so much better than human wisdom because it is "peaceable, gentle, reasonable, full of mercy and good fruits, unwavering, without hypocrisy" (James 3:17), as opposed to our own wisdom, which is laced with pain, pride, and selfish motives.

Think about King Solomon, who grew up in a troubled home. He learned about his father's strengths and weaknesses from the psalms. No doubt, being the son of King David, Solomon heard these songs of God's mercy, love, trust, and integrity in his formative years. His reliance upon God probably grew out of hearing stories of his father's victory over the Philistine giant, Goliath. The young man's understanding of God's forgiveness came from the recounting of his father's sin with his mother, Bathsheba.

David probably sang about these things to his son. Just imagine this boy sitting at his father's feet, soaking up the truths about God. Solomon's father was known for being a man after God's own heart. It was from this upbringing that our young king made an important request of God.

Facing the responsibility of ruling God's people after his father's death, God asked the new king, Solomon, what he could give him. The young ruler responded by requesting "an understanding heart to judge Your people to discern between good and evil" (1 Kings 3:9). This young man recognized the enormity of his responsibility as king, as well as his own weaknesses and deficiencies. Solomon knew it would take wisdom from God to accomplish the task at hand. He also knew God loved the people he was appointed to rule and judge.

Think about Solomon's wise request for just a second. Our young ruler wanted more than just success as a good king who made good decisions—he wanted God's best for God's people, and he was aware of the age-old battle between good and evil.

Soon after Harvey and I were married, we realized bringing our family together would be a big job. Like the young king, we were overwhelmed by not only the responsibility but the resistance and bad attitudes coming from the kids. We knew it would take God's wisdom to pull it off. We, too, asked God for wisdom and an understanding heart to see past our own emotions in order to do what is best for the children, who were being split between households.

Solomon's wisdom was tested almost immediately when two prostitutes came before him with a "child custody" case. One woman related the story to Solomon how they had lived together, each having a newborn son. During the night, one woman rolled over on her baby, killing him, while the other mother lay sleeping with her child. The woman with the dead child got up and switched the babies. When the unsuspecting mother woke up to feed her baby the next morning, he was dead. On closer examination she realized that it wasn't her baby. Both women claimed the living child. Solomon had to determine who the real mother was and give her custody. Everyone was watching and waiting to see what this young, inexperienced king would do.

Solomon did the unexpected. He called for a sword to cut the child in half. He said he would divide the child and give half to each woman. Can you just imagine the faces in that room? The first woman pleaded with the king to let the child live, willingly giving up her parental rights to the other woman for the child's sake. The other woman was perfectly happy to go with the king's judgment to divide the child in two. The real mother's heart was revealed in her willingness to sacrifice for the sake of her son—the child was given to her in one piece.

Everyone in the nation of Israel was amazed by Solomon's wisdom. He displayed an understanding heart by appealing to a mother's love for her child. I think many of us with children who are being torn between two households can relate to the mother's dilemma in Solomon's story. Like Solomon, God appeals to our parental love for the decisions we make concerning our children. He also wants to give us an understanding heart to discern between good and evil—or in our case, emotional confusion over visitation and the turbulent permanent wave.

My understanding heart was formed as I sought the Lord to help me see past my own emotions. It didn't just drop down into my chest in one fell swoop; it came gradually. By putting the children's emotional needs before my own, one disrupted plan after another and one bad attitude at a time, I could more clearly see what was happening to my stepchildren when they came home from visitation.

Standing in the whirlwind of mixed emotions that accompany visitation, it's easy to lose our footing and our vision. Our eyes stray from the importance of living out our Christian faith in love. We tend to look at the aggravation of dealing with the ex, rejection from the kids, and even competition for our spouse's love. Our vision is clouded by our emotions and our overwhelming circumstances.

Although we may feel as if we are "being put to death all day long," God does offer hope. The Bible says nothing will separate us from the love of Christ (see Rom. 8:38–39). He is right there with us, interceding on our behalf. If we keep our eyes on Jesus, like a lighthouse in a storm, we will have the clear vision to find solid ground rather than the crashing waves of splitting the child in visitation.

SPLITTING THE CHILD: TWO FAMILIES/TWO SETS OF RULES

"Mom doesn't make me go to church." "Dad lets me stay up as late as I want to." "I don't have to do chores at Mom's!" "I'm allowed to watch these movies at Mom's house." "My dad says I don't have to do what you say because you're not my father!"

Do any of these quips sound familiar? If you're a parent in a blended family, they probably do. Not only do the words ring a bell, but the attitudes that accompany them reverberate like a gong, leaving us all a little dizzy.

If my stepchildren ever wanted to set me off, one of the "Mom lets me . . ." phrases would do the job. It felt as if my husband's ex-wife was challenging me and my parental authority on a daily basis, without ever setting foot into our home. Instead of taking a discerning look at the conflicting emotions the kids were experiencing while living in two households, I thought it was all about me. Overwhelmed by feelings of rejection, I added fuel to the already flammable mix of emotions with my angry and resentful responses. Not surprisingly, explosions frequently erupted, leaving the kids even more insecure and confused than ever. Because of this, I needed help with my responses.

Because we want to teach our children good habits and train them up to be responsible adults, we set up house rules, bedtimes, homework schedules, etc., based on our values. In the biological family, there may be a little rebellion concerning the rules from time to time, but for the most part they are accepted. In the blended family, however, this setup is only half of the child's life. They have another household and another set of rules that may or may not be based on the same values we hold. Unlike the child in Solomon's story, our children *are* actually being split in two. The sword of visitation may not be crafted of steel like Solomon's, but its blade is every bit as cold and sharp.

Drawing this sword and splitting a child could destroy him, so how does one peaceably divide a living, breathing child between households? Solomon prayed for wisdom. His prayer yielded a discernment to see past the two mothers' obvious display of emotion over the one living child. If prayer yielded a -discerning heart for Solomon, we have to assume this would be a great starting place for anyone splitting a child.

Seeing past what *we* want in our immediate situation, especially when it is fueled by emotions, is very difficult. Solomon's ridiculous solution to draw a sword jolted the mother into seeing a bigger picture. The importance of the argument at hand dimmed in comparison to her child's well-being. All of a sudden, having her way wasn't the most important thing.

ADJUSTMENT ALLOWANCES

When a child makes a transition between households, he or she feels the change of rules and, sometimes values, immediately. Our children often meet this transition with bad attitudes and resentments. When our children return to our home, we feel relieved that the ball is now back in our court. As parents, we expect our kids to bounce right back into our way of doing things—and do it with a smile.

If the kids only live with us a short period of time, we want to make the most of it. However, in order for our children to feel like they are part of our family, we have to allow them time to gradually work or fit into family routines. Our children may not even know why they are in such a foul mood, or why they are being difficult when they come home. The children are just in the transition period. Give them a little time to make the adjustment, and you'll soon see tensions relax.

Time of adjustment between households can vary. The longer the time of separation and the further apart our values are from the other parents', the longer the adjustment period.

Harvey and I noticed that the girls had a pattern of behavior following each visitation. A bad attitude and a maddening silence always climbed into the van with the girls. Something just wasn't natural about three little girls sitting quietly for an hour and a half drive. The silence weighed our van down more than all of their luggage combined.

Harvey usually tried to break the mood by asking them if they had a good weekend. The snappy one-word answers prompted him to ask another question, like, "What did you do?" He wasn't trying to pry into life at their mother's house; he was just trying to lighten the air by making conversation. Innocent as Harvey's questions were, they were perceived as a challenge by the girls. Discerning between good and evil was the farthest thing from our minds, so the explosive dialogue that followed made for a miserable ride home.

Confronting the girls about their attitudes only pushed them farther away from us. We realized that breaking out of this pattern would require God's help. My husband and I prayed about it, and Harvey came up with a simple solution. The plan was to get past the attitudes by doing and saying nothing. This was an adjustment period.

You see, we knew what to expect when we picked up the girls—an attitude manifested by silence. Harvey's plan was to pick up the girls, ask no questions, and just talk about what a great weekend *we* had. This diverted the attention off of them and their mother and onto neutral ground. The only question we asked them was if they were hungry—they were always ready to eat. By ignoring their silence and making our own conversation, the girls' attitudes relaxed, allowing a pleasant ride home. After about a day and a half, they were always back to their old selves again.

THE LAND OF OZ: FANTASY VISITATIONS AND THE RETURN TO KANSAS

Remember Dorothy from the classic movie *The Wizard of Oz*? After stepping outside of her own gray world, Dorothy found herself in the wonderment of Oz. Oz was a place where everything was colorful, bright, and happy—a direct contrast to her drab life in Kansas. Our children sometimes feel they have traveled over the rainbow to Oz when their noncustodial parent showers them with gifts and fun times during their stay. These fantasy visitations are great fun for the kids while they last, but the inevitable return to Kansas may leave them disillusioned with their life at home.

A child assumes if they lived with the other parent, they would get to do fun things all the time. Their mom or dad would buy them anything they wanted, anytime they wanted it. Of course, everyone else knows this would not be the case, but the child still feels let down when he comes home.

Giving extravagant gifts to your children and taking them on fun excursions is a real temptation for the noncustodial parent. Harvey and I were even guilty of this to a certain extent before we gained custody of the girls. We took advantage of every opportunity to give to our children. Every other weekend, we went go-carting or to movies with all the kids. We felt guilty over the fact that we weren't able to parent them consistently, which gave way to unbalanced parenting.

My children, living with us full-time, couldn't understand why we never did anything fun unless the girls came. This imbalance in our parenting caused my children to resent the girls because it seemed as if they weren't as important to us as Harvey's children.

After Harvey and I saw that the other kids were resenting the "special treatment" the girls were expecting and receiving, we decided to reevaluate our weekend visitations. By restricting our excursions to just an occasional trip to the go-cart track or the movies, they became special times for the whole family. A by-product of this new balance was the quality time we spent as a family at home. The kids did things together, such as riding bikes, jumping on the trampoline, or just drawing pictures. They grew accustomed to normal life at home, which later made the custody transition easier for them.

Whether or not you are the custodial parent, your child should be your most important consideration. Ask yourself a few questions:

1. If my child lived with me full-time, would I give him these gifts or do the same activities with him as often as I do now?

2. Is my child *expecting* to be showered with these gifts?

3. Does he *expect* me to take him somewhere fun every time I am with him?

4. Does my child measure how much I love him by what I give him and where I take him?

5. Do I feel guilty if I don't fill our time together with special things?

If the answer to any of these questions is yes, you may need to balance out your visitation with more quality time at home. We want to teach our children the value of time and money. Our children will learn to appreciate both of these values when we set an example for them to follow.

Looking back, Harvey and I can see how our fantasy-land visits left a false sense of how life would be living with us on a full-time basis. As a result of reevaluating our weekends and making a few changes, our time with both sets of children became fairly consistent.

Kansas

You may be on the Kansas end of the rainbow. Perhaps your child comes back from a weekend in Oz to an ordinary, gray world of homework, chores, and bedtime. These things are just a normal part of life, but how do you compete with the colorful world of Oz? After all, your child never hears their weekend parent say, "Get ready for school!"

You may not have control over what the other parent does with your child, but you can make the transition easier by having a cheerful attitude when your child comes home. Arguing with your ex or verbalizing to your child how wrong their other parent is only drives a wedge in your relationship with him or her. If your child is excited about the weekend, share in the joy instead of scowling in disapproval. Allow him or her enough time for adjustment back into your routines, and remember Dorothy's ending sentiment about Kansas and Oz: "There's no place like home."

BAD REPORTS

In the blended family, where children are split between two households, parents sometimes want to know what goes on in the other household. Consequently, when our kids come back from visitation with a bad attitude toward us, we conveniently blame the other parent for planting bad seeds in their minds.

When parents fish for information, their child may feel more acceptance by obliging them with a report. Reports can be about anything and everything: conversations, changes in home décor, visitors, meal preparations, chores, punishments, how one cleans house or drives a car—nothing is private.

Some children are so eager to please, they exaggerate arguments with their stepparent or emphasize their negative attributes. Tensions run high, and everyone gets pulled into a game of tug-of-war. Because our children are the rope in this game, they end up frayed, stretched to their limits, and broken. This game has no winners.

If they show too much joy over seeing the stepparent at the time of exchange, or even if they appear to like them, our children may feel they are betraying their biological parent. Often, where dissention exists between the exes, the kids can be drawn into negative conversations about their parents. Talking about a child's other parent in a negative light is one of Satan's schemes to breed contempt. This is why it is important to take a hard look at the way we talk to our kids and the questions we ask them concerning their mom or dad.

Although it is impossible to control what goes on in the other household, we can limit the reporting in our own home. Instead of responding with probing questions when bits of information are offered, we can let the subject drop. Check the motives behind your questions. Don't get caught up in the trap of using your children to get to your ex, even if the child is willing. Once the child sees that you aren't playing that game, they will stop playing it as well. The tidbits of information gained in this way only teach our children to pit one parent against the other.

Send a clear message to your children that your love and affirmation have nothing to do with what goes on in the other parent's household. A child should never feel he has to earn your love and affection by betraying someone else—especially not their other parent. The ones who suffer the most in hostilities between divorced parents are the children. Give your child less to report by implementing the closed-door rule and by not talking about the other parent.

THE JUGGLING ACT:
HOLIDAYS, VACATIONS, AND SPECIAL EVENTS

Have you ever watched a juggler? He tosses several balls into the air, effortlessly catching and tossing them over and over again. A good juggler never drops a ball. He makes it seem so easy, as if anyone could do it. I've even seen jugglers spin plates while tossing balls, but guess what? If I tried that, I'd drop the ball every time, and my plates would come crashing to the floor in a million pieces. Why? Because I never learned to balance the rise and fall of the balls with my hands and eyes, much less add a spinning plate to the mix. I did, however, learn to juggle holidays, vacations, and special events with fairly reasonable balance.

The first and most important thing to consider when planning events is the reason you are doing it. For example, your purpose for planning a family vacation is to enjoy a special time together as a family. The purpose for planning a special dinner and gift exchange at Christmas is to celebrate Christ's birth with your family. If you are planning a special event such as a wedding or graduation, the purpose is to honor the graduate or the bride and groom. With the purpose understood, the second thing to consider, for our children's sake, is the best way to plan the event with the least amount of conflict.

The easiest way to plan family holidays is to find out what the other parent's plans are first. There is nothing more irritating than having to rearrange all your plans after they have been set in motion. You'll find it to be far less stressful if you remain flexible whenever possible, rather than insisting on having the kids home by a certain day or time.

Holidays, vacations, and special events are big in our family. Doing the family thing has always been a lot of fun for us, but planning it hasn't. My calendar had every weekend marked with either an **H** for Harvey's weekend or a letter indicating his ex-spouse's initial. We were always careful to make our plans on the **H** weekends. Holidays and vacations were another matter. Although visitation times were clearly written out in the custody agreement, special trips, holidays, or events sometimes required communication with Harvey's ex-wife to work out special details or to trade weekends.

Once I knew the arrangements of the holiday visitation, planning our family time went much smoother. Special meals for holidays like Easter, Thanksgiving, and Christmas were planned a little later than normal to allow for a possible late arrival after the exchange. We did our best to make sure the children didn't have to miss out on anything.

Some families have traditions, such as celebrating Christmas on Christmas Eve; but if the kids can't be a part of it, the purpose of having a "family holiday" is lost. The same is true for those who celebrate only on Christmas morning. Over the years, we have opened gifts on Christmas morning, Christmas night, Christmas Eve, and even the day after Christmas. The important thing is not to make an issue of when as much as *why* and *who*.

Think about your family ten years down the road. What will stick in your child's mind when they think of holidays and special events? Laughter, surprises, and great food around the family table? These make a much better memory than arguments between parents. What do you want your child's memories of Christmas holidays, vacations, graduations, or birthdays to be? It won't matter ten years from now whose turn it was to have Christmas Eve with the kids or the injustice you may have felt over giving up a weekend to have a two-week vacation with them. What children will remember, however, is their parents always arguing over or during the times that should have been fun. Allowing arguments to color your special events has the same crashing result as the juggler who gets out of balance by dropping the ball.

COMPROMISE:
BITTER MEDICINE FOR HEALTHY FAMILIES

I liken the word *compromise* to taking a spoonful of disgusting medicine. When I'm feeling ill, I put off taking the murky liquid as long as possible. Thoughts of swallowing and choking down the bitter remedy overshadow my common sense. Of course I know the medicine is going to make me feel better—I just don't like how it tastes going down or the aftertaste it leaves in my mouth. Compromising on our holiday traditions or vacation plans can have a bitter taste as well. Hard as it might be to swallow, compromise does benefit our family as a whole. Don't forget—the purpose is not to have our own way or even our traditions; it is to celebrate the holiday or event as a family.

Young King Solomon sat at his father's feet and learned from him. What will your children learn from your example? Like most parents in blended families, Harvey and I had to give up something nearly every time we planned a special event or holiday. Compromise is a part of life for anyone in a blended family, but it can actually be palatable if family unity accompanies it. Family unity, after all, *is* what we are trying to achieve in tying our family knot.

Anticipation is half the fun in the Christmas preparations. One year when the girls were about seven, eight, and nine years old, our Christmas holiday was dampened by the fact that we would not have them here for the weeks leading up to Christmas. In fact, they would not be with us until late afternoon on Christmas Day. My children's ages were twelve, -fifteen, and eighteen at the time. We had this anticipation with my children, but the girls' absence left a hole in our holiday. They weren't there when the decorations went up or when the Christmas cookies were baked. They didn't see the beautifully wrapped gifts piling up for them under the tree, and we couldn't tease them about being naughty or nice.

In a perfect world our whole family would be together Christmas morning—getting up early, reading the Christmas story together, and then opening gifts. My children expected to do those things because they had been at home the whole time, anticipating the excitement of Christmas morning. We didn't want them to feel cheated by having to wait for the girls to arrive, but we didn't want the girls to feel left out if we didn't wait for them. We faced a dilemma in trying to figure out how and when we could open gifts. Harvey and I turned over several ideas, but there didn't seem to be a suitable compromise.

In situations like this, we can easily lose sight of the purpose of our celebration and focus on the negative. I wanted to fight for my children's right to enjoy a fun Christmas morning, and Harvey wanted to fight for his children's right to be a part of the family. Once we took a hard look at the big picture, we concluded that even though the girls didn't live with us and weren't with us in the weeks leading up to the holiday, they needed to feel as if they were a part of our family's Christmas celebration. We also wanted my children to include the girls, even though they wouldn't be able to share in the holiday until the very end. The compromise we finally reached had to have come from the Lord—it was too perfect not to.

We decided to build a tree house for the girls as a special Christmas gift. Harvey, Jeremy, and Aaron did all the work on the tree house project while Jennifer and I stood on the overlooking deck "supervising," adding our two cents and creative opinions on how it should be built. By focusing our attention on this special project for the girls, our whole family was unified in the holiday celebration. We knew the girls would be excited about having a fun hideaway, complete with porthole windows and a rope ladder. Because the tree house would be the girl's big gift from all of us, we decided to allow my kids to enjoy their gift exchange on Christmas morning, as they always had.

When the girls arrived that afternoon, none of us could wait to see their faces when they saw the tree house. They were thrilled. With all the excitement over the unveiling of the tree house and opening the rest of their gifts, they never felt as if they weren't part of our Christmas. What could have been our most miserable holiday became one of our most memorable.

THE BIG PICTURE

When you are in the midst of changing diapers and kissing boo-boos, childhood may seem like an eternity, but blink once or twice and your kids will be grown. The time we spend with our kids is much too valuable to squander it on arguments and issues that contribute nothing to their character development and confidence as young adults. Whether you have custody of your children or not, make the time you spend with them count.

Our children are our most precious treasures on this earth. Visitation is one of the most emotionally challenging situations your child can possibly face. We can make riding the turbulent permanent wave easier if our children don't have to deal with strife between the two people they love most—mom and dad.

When you and your ex are at an impasse, stop, pray, and remember the mother in Solomon's story. Readjust your scope of vision to see the big picture. What is best for your child? Put your trust in a loving God to give you an understanding heart. He cares more about your kids than you could ever imagine.

Your family knot will hold secure when you are fair and consistent. Looking back, I've tried to remember specific compromises we made. But guess what? Recalling those details is difficult because my memories are of the great times we shared as a family. By placing the priority on our purpose rather than on having our own way, the good times, not the details of the compromises, have stuck in everyone's memory. Difficult as it might be to relinquish control, remind yourself of how your child feels being a rope split in two in a game of tug-of-war. Remember, the objective is to tie your family knot together—not pull it apart.

Chapter Eleven

BEFORE YOU HIRE
AN ATTORNEY

He is a shield to those who walk in integrity,
Guarding the paths of justice.
~ Proverbs 2:7–8

Do you remember the first time you gazed upon your newborn child? I do. Everyone told me my baby's face was all scrunched up and purple looking. Some even said he looked like a little old man! Jeremy may have been a little scrawny and purple at four and a half pounds (having been born early), but I saw something completely different than everyone else. Maybe it was the long labor and the lack of an epidural, but I saw a perfectly beautiful baby. My son was a handsome little child with bright eyes, ten fingers, and ten toes—it was love at first sight.

Nothing compares to a parent's love for their children. The smallest signs of growth and development are often shouted from the rooftops. I recorded every little burp and gurgle in my son's baby book. You might think me a little strange, but I even kept the dried-up umbilical cord as a connection between me and my firstborn. Everything changed the day he was born. In fact, I can actually break up my life into old and new testaments—BC and AC: Before Children and After Children.

I love my children, and I want what is best for them—at least that's what I tell myself. Love compels parents to do all sorts of things for their children. Daddy imagines his new baby boy growing up to follow in his footsteps. He has his son's life planned out for him before the little guy even takes his first step. In his mind's eye, he sees "Clark & Son" on the sign above the family business. Mommy enters her little daughter in all the "beautiful baby" contests because she sees her baby girl growing up to be Miss America one day.

Before you become too alarmed by my examples, think back to when your child was a baby. Did you buy camouflage for your baby boy because daddy likes to hunt? Did baby girl get a toy piano for Christmas because mommy's passion is music? When Jennifer was only two, I bought her a toy sewing machine because I liked to sew. The first thing she did was prick her finger on the needle like Sleeping Beauty, and that was the last time she ever even came close to a sewing machine. Because having children constitutes one of life's greatest blessings, let's not come under too much condemnation for wanting our kids to be like us. We want to shower our children with the things we love and enjoy in life.

Love for our children motivates many of the major decisions parents make in life. We buy a house based on the school district, we buy a car with a high safety rating to protect our children, and we even turn down good-paying jobs because they take too much time from the children. Many divorced or widowed mothers and fathers even reject potential spouses on the basis of what their children think. Unfortunately, parental love can at times cloud our vision to what is truly best for our children.

In a blended family where children are split between parents, *both* parents think they know what is best, and *both* feel passionately about it. Conflicts often surface because what one parent thinks is best for his or her child can be wildly different from what the other parent thinks. Arguments, charged with negative emotions, can surround our children. Sadly, in the heat of the battle, the kids become pawns in a game of parental chess.

One parent may feel they need more visitation time, but the custodial parent refuses to permit it. Another parent may demand to know how their child support is being spent, while the custodial parent insists it is none of their business. A custodial parent may be living under a heavy financial burden, so the noncustodial parent is convinced their child would be better off living with them. When parents are at odds over their children or issues involving them, the most common solution is to take it to the next level—court.

The question we must honestly ask ourselves is this: Is going to court the best thing for our children? Will they be better off, or will we? Stepping into court is like stepping into a muddy chasm. Once you take the first step, you will get your shoes muddy and alter the landscape of your home.

MUDDY SHOES

Lately Harvey and I have been doing a lot of work to the outside of our home. We poured a new patio, built a cover over it, and then, to carry out the Southwestern theme of our home, we laid Spanish-style, terra-cotta tiles. Sealing the grout in the tile was the only thing left to do on our patio. Everything was looking great, but our tired old yard still needed a facelift. So while the work on the tile was nearing completion, Harvey commissioned some landscaping to be done in the yard.

Our backyard was a flurry of activity; work crews were dumping and spreading dirt, edging and shaping flowerbeds, and digging an irrigation system. Everything was going well—until a downpour of rain abruptly brought all the work to a stop.

After the weekend rain, I went out onto the patio to talk to a worker who was standing at the far end of the backyard. He was having trouble hearing me, so without thinking, I stepped off the newly tiled patio into the dirt that had been dumped and spread just before the rain. At least, I *thought* I was stepping off the patio into the dirt; instead, I found myself sinking into about four or five inches of mud.

Once I took the first steps into the mud, I was committed—there was no turning back. If I did turn back onto the patio with my mud-covered tennis shoes, the unsealed grout around the new tile would be ruined. To make matters worse, I just happened to be wearing my brand-new white tennis shoes, purchased just the day before.

The prospect of taking several more steps in that thick, sticky mud was daunting, but Harvey and I had too much invested in the unsealed tile to risk messing it up—I had no choice but to go forward. With brown goo seeping up to the tops of my new shoes and a disgusting sucking noise accompanying every step, I trudged my way through the future flower garden.

Once I reached the solid ground and green grass on the other side, I turned around to survey the damage. My new shoes were covered in mud, and an obvious trail of deep, foot-shaped impressions was left in the once smooth ground behind me. I certainly regretted ever taking that first step. My muddy shoes and the mess I'd made of the landscape work made me wish I had taken a closer look at what I was getting into *before* stepping off the patio.

What is the moral of this story? Don't wear new shoes in the mud? Of course, but the lesson goes even deeper. This tale proves you must know what you are getting into before you take that first step, particularly in litigation or judicial battles over your children. You may think you're stepping onto fairly solid ground, only to find yourself sinking into a muddy mess. Sometimes it is far better to find another way around your differences with your ex than going to court because the damage to your children and family may far outweigh your need to enter litigation in the first place.

Though there are a lot of legitimate reasons to go to court with an ex-spouse, there are just as many reasons not to. This is one of those really *big* decisions—one that requires doing some research and asking some hard questions. Whatever your intention might be—whether it's custody change, collecting back child support, enforcing visitation, or even enforcing previous court rulings—I advise you and your spouse to spend some serious time in prayer and then examine all the costs and risks together.

Ask questions of friends and acquaintances who have had courtroom experience. Seek counseling. Talk and pray about it as husband and wife. Are you both ready for the effects litigation will have on your marriage emotionally, financially, and even spiritually? Will the end result of litigation be worth the cost to your family? Will your children suffer more from the trauma of a court battle than if things stayed as they are? Apart from the obvious love you have for your children, there are many things to consider, examine, and pray about before you hire an attorney.

Going to court is a very big decision, so take a real good look at the ground *before* you get your shoes muddy and tear up the landscape. You might just decide the mud in front of you is too deep, and you're better off finding another way around to the green grass on the other side.

Examining the Ground

It would have been nice to have had a measuring stick to test the depth and ooze factor of the mud before taking a stroll through my legal landscape. To help you to measure the solidity of your legal ground, I've devised a simple three-point test you and your spouse can take together. These questions will probe a little deeper—past your love for your child—to determine if this landscape is something you really want to get into. Measure your circumstances and reasons for entering litigation with your ex-spouse by looking closely at three things: motive, means, and method. Honestly ask and answer all these questions together with your spouse.

1. *Motive*: What is your primary reason for going to court? Are you doing it for the child or for yourself? Have you considered how a court battle will affect your child? Will the trauma to your child do more harm than leaving things as they are or possibly finding an alternate solution?

2. *Means*: Do you have the means to go the distance if the battle drags on over an extended period of time? Do you have plenty of spiritual, emotional, financial, and marital resources from which to draw? Is your spouse behind you 100 percent? Litigation will tax more than just your finances.

3. *Method*: Do you have a plan? Is it your plan or God's? Are you willing to be flexible to God's leading, or have you decided what you will do, without wavering? Have you considered all your options aside from going to court?

Examine your motive, means, and method by spending time communicating with your spouse and with God. Together, you should be able to determine whether or not to stay on the patio or trudge in the mud.

If you do decide to go trudging, spiritually anchor yourself to the solid Rock of Jesus Christ. He will help you and your spouse to make it through all of the legal pitfalls, lawyers, judges, and an impersonal court system. The ground is incredibly slippery, and without Christ I wouldn't advise taking that first step.

MOTIVE

Apart from your legal reasons for hiring an attorney, you must ask yourself who you are doing it for—you or your child? This is where the mud gets a little thick and sticky.

The question of motive remains at the top of our measuring stick because it constitutes the one thing we, as followers of Jesus Christ, must continually ask ourselves at every level of life and in everything we do. David cried out to God in Psalm 139:23–24, saying, "Search me, O God, and know my heart; Try me and know my anxious thoughts; and see if there be any hurtful way in me, and lead me in the way everlasting." Jeremiah made a similar plea to God in Jeremiah 12:3: "But You know me, O LORD, You see me; and You examine my heart's attitude toward You." Even Paul, on several occasions made reference to examining one's heart and motive (1 Cor. 11:28; 2 Cor. 13:5; Gal. 6:4). He sums it up neatly in 1 Thessalonians 5:21–22: "But examine everything carefully; hold fast to that which is good; abstain from every form of evil."

Obviously, we aren't trying to do something evil when we go to court. We hire an attorney to help us do what we feel is best for our children. In doing this, however, our choices should stem from an honest heart open to God's leading—rather than a heart bent on revenge or resentment toward our ex. Additionally, we should consider the effect our decision will have on our children, because we don't want them to be wounded in the battle.

If love's the only motivation in seeking custody, consider looking beyond your own desire: What is the best thing for *your child?* Remember, he or she has already, in his or her young life, been through some traumatic experiences. His world was turned upside down when his parents divorced.

If you are reading this book, chances are you have remarried, so the child also has experienced his mom or dad's world change. He is adjusting to a stepparent and possibly step-siblings, a new set of grandparents, maybe a new home, a new school, and a new life. Too often, children of divorce are put in the middle of arguments and hostilities between their parents—two people they love more than anyone else in the world. Going to court only adds to a child's feelings of insecurity and instability.

Ask yourself some basic questions and answer them truthfully from your heart. Can your child emotionally handle being put through another traumatic experience? Does the situation surrounding your child warrant a court battle?

If you are considering a custody change, is your child at risk or in danger? Before you answer, let's define danger and risk. A dangerous situation is one involving physical or sexual abuse of the child. A risk involves neglect of the child's welfare: living with a parent addicted to drugs or alcohol, or being exposed to illegal activity or potentially dangerous people, or just being left alone. In cases where abuse or neglect is present, you should try to get your child out of that environment.

Risk can be, but isn't necessarily, defined as a child living with a parent who loves them but is financially insecure. Many parents seek custody of their children just because they can provide a better life for their child. Children who live in a home where money is tight are not at risk. If you are worried about issues like health insurance and clothes, few custodial parents will object to receiving additional child support. However, new clothes and bikes are a poor substitute for a mom or dad who loves them.

For some parents, money is a big reason they go to court to win custody of their children. Perhaps paying child support every week puts a strain on their wallet. On the opposite side of the coin, perhaps custody is seen as a means to *get* child support. They really need the extra money. This is where we want to reexamine our motives. We don't want to put our need for money before our child's best interest. If we follow God's principles for living, our needs will be met.

Pray about your decision to go to court and be sure your motives are pure and honest. Be certain your spouse is 100 percent behind you and both of you understand what kind of mud you're about to step into. Trudging through mud in the new white shoes of marriage is a very unpleasant experience. But if you know in your heart that this is what God is leading you to do, and you have the right motives, by all means, move to the next stage of our test.

MEANS

Examining means is the middle mark on our measuring stick. When I discuss *means,* I'm not talking exclusively about finances, although finances are necessary in any legal matter. What I am referring to is you and your spouse's emotional, spiritual, and marital resources, as well as your time. Not just the time from filing to judgment, but the time required for ongoing appeals. For many, it is never really *over* until your children turn eighteen. Court will cost you—more than just money.

My friend Linda had no idea what she and her new husband, Mike, were getting into when they tried to get custody of Mike's young daughter, Tiffany. In their case, the child was in danger and the mother was hostile. Linda had an idea of what Mike's ex-wife was like before they married, but she never imagined the full extent of what she was walking into when she said, "I do."

When Linda and Mike filed for a custody change, Mike's ex-wife called and harassed each of them at their jobs. They had to get an unlisted phone number at home. Linda said they were always looking over their shoulder and worried about what Cassie, Mike's ex-wife, might do next. She had already smashed and vandalized Linda's car on more than one occasion, even pouring sugar into her gas tank while the car was parked at her mother's house.

These were small things compared to Cassie's drug and alcohol addictions. She had a constant stream of men sleeping over, and Mike and Linda were worried about Tiffany's safety. Whenever they had visitation with little Tiffany, she looked as if she hadn't been bathed in a long time, and it appeared that her diaper hadn't been changed regularly.

Linda's heart went out to Tiffany, and she was in full agreement with Mike as they did what they could to bring her home. They prayed together daily for Tiffany's protection and for God to give them custody.

In a recent conversation with Linda, she said something that really struck home with me. She said, "We naively assumed that because we were Christians, we would win." Linda went on to explain how she and Mike just *knew* that the lawyers and judges would see through Cassie's façade of motherhood. However, in court Cassie always looked perfectly normal, so when Mike and Linda's attorney made accusations of Cassie's bizarre behavior, it was met with a lukewarm response.

In most cases, before a judge will take a child away from his or her mother or change a custody ruling, there must be a significant change in circumstances. The mother must be proven to be unfit, or it has to be shown that the child is in danger.

Mike and Linda knew what was going on, but convincing the judge was another matter. Even after Cassie went to jail on drug charges and was found in contempt of court, Linda and Mike had trouble getting the courts to enforce the rulings.

Linda told me that she and Mike realized that yes, maybe they were both Christians, but lawyers, judges, and court systems operate according to the world's standards—and we live in a fallen world. Linda told me that they lost more court battles with Cassie than they won. The judicial system put their faith, finances, and new marriage to the test.

Linda recounted her feelings of betrayal in this first year of marriage as their legal drama unfolded. She had waited until she was thirty-nine to marry, and she felt that she had finally found her prince charming. Her joy, however, turned to anger as the mud slinging intensified. Linda lost a measure of respect for her new husband because she couldn't understand how he could have married Cassie in the first place, much less have a child with her. Linda acknowledges now that in her frustration and disappointment she was trying to play God in Mike's life, condemning him for his past mistakes.

In the end, full custody and guardianship rights were given to Mike and Linda. Their marriage survived because of their commitment to their wedding vows and their total reliance on God's grace to see them through it. Though they've reached the solid ground on the other side of the landscape, they are still cleaning mud off their new shoes.

METHOD

Putting faith and trust in God is the best method for success in every area of blending our families, including court battles. Hebrews 11:1 defines faith like this: "Now faith is the assurance of things hoped for, the conviction of things not seen." If we could *see* the thing we are hoping for, it wouldn't require us to call on God for help. When we put our children in God's hands, the circumstances may not have changed, but our conviction has. Instead of relying on attorneys, judges, private investigators, and ourselves, we are relying on an all-knowing God who can part the seas and change the heart of man.

Both Harvey and I can testify in our own custody case that it wasn't until we released everything into God's hands that we won the ultimate victory. God's method is always better than our own.

If Harvey and I weren't on the phone, we were in and out of attorneys' offices. We did a lot of the legwork for the attorney—some necessary and some because we wanted to be sure all the bases were covered. The custody case consumed our lives. Our method of gaining victory was to draw from the hip and shoot at anything that moved.

While in the midst of litigation, it is easy to focus on the depth of the mud and the distance yet to trudge. Human nature drives us to take matters into our own hands, losing sight of God. Our plan or method always seems to be the best to us. We like being in control, especially when it comes to the children we love.

Harvey and I justified our actions by reasoning that if we didn't do all we could, we might lose the girls—we were doing it for them. In reality, our efforts were putting a strain on our new marriage, our family, our finances, and our walk with God. Not only that, our daughters were feeling excessive pressure from both households.

As long as we held onto the reins, God wasn't in control—Harvey and I were. We were getting nowhere, fast. Finally, after wearing ourselves out trying to make things happen in our case, we released control to God.

Ceasing all of our activities, Harvey and I turned to God, laying our concerns for the girls at his feet. We decided that God loved them even more than we did, and if it was his will for the girls to live with us, he would make it happen.

Almost immediately after we turned the whole thing over to God, things began to change. Through an unexpected turn of events, we went back to court and won custody. We didn't have to do a thing or spend any more money. God was in control.

God's motivation for moving on our behalf was love—the same motivation you have for moving on your children's behalf. God's love is completely pure and unconditional. Jesus proclaimed, "If you then, being evil, know how to give good gifts to your children, how much more will your Father who is in heaven give what is good to those who ask Him!" (Matt. 7:11).

We must follow *God's* plan if we expect our home to stand. Think about this: would your children benefit if you won your case, only to put them through another divorce? God's ways are much better than ours.

MUD PUDDLES: AN ATTORNEY'S ADVICE

Now that you and your spouse have measured motive, means, and method by taking the three-point test, and you've determined that going to court is the only viable solution in your situation, it is time to get some legal advice.

In an effort to look out for your "new shoes," I have trudged ahead of you just a step or two to possibly provide an advantage in getting around the hidden pitfalls of the legal system. I'm no expert in legal matters, so I talked with an attorney who specializes in family law to get a broader perspective of the mud puddles commonly associated with domestic disputes between ex-spouses.

Attorney Michelle Strause, with the Farrar Firm in Hot Springs, Arkansas, has represented clients in every kind of family dispute, including divorce, custody, child support, and visitation. Strause has specialized in family law for seventeen years, including being a court-appointed "attorney ad lidem"—an attorney representing the best interests of children whose divorced parents can't agree. I asked her to give me the court's perspective of cases between ex-spouses involving children.

Ms. Strause said that the moment parents enter into divorce, they lose a measure of control over their children for the rest of their children's minor years. The judge determines which parent will have custody of the child, how much child support should be paid by the noncustodial parent, and how, when, and if visitation rights will be exercised. Because parents have different ideas about what is best for their children, a judge examines all the information presented to him by both parties and from the attorney ad lidem, if one was appointed. The judge then makes the ruling *he* believes is in the child's best interest.

If you are in a blended family, you have obviously experienced a judge's determination on child custody, visitation, and child support. If you're reading this chapter, you may be thinking about seeking a change in the judge's ruling on one or more of these issues regarding your child. Ms. Strause states that a judge's ruling can always be modified. In fact, in her experience as an attorney, Ms. Strause has seen many rulings changed. While some were good for the children, far too many were not. In those cases, the parent may have won, but the child ultimately lost.

COMMON MISCONCEPTIONS

I asked Ms. Strause to explain some of the common misconceptions parents entering litigation might have, particularly when seeking a custody change. For instance, many parents think that when a child turns twelve or thirteen, they can choose which parent to live with. She clarified this misunderstanding for us by explaining the legal process of making a change in a judge's ruling.

The child's best interest is *always* first and foremost in the judge's mind. When a child reaches a certain age—generally ranging between twelve to fifteen years—the courts do place increased emphasis on the child's preference of where they want to live. Nonetheless, the courts still look at a number of variables to determine if a change of custody should occur.

For example, a fourteen-year-old daughter wants to go live with daddy because she knows that the rules, curfews, and boundaries established in mom's home will not be enforced at dad's house. Although her preference will be taken into consideration, the courts will be looking at the child's best interest. The judge will examine carefully both households to determine if there has been a significant change of circumstances to warrant a custody change.

Ms. Strause explained that a variety of changes could affect a judge's decision: if the custodial parent has gone through a divorce, if there is violence in the home, severe financial difficulties, or severe difficulty controlling the child. A child simply *wanting* to live with the other parent isn't a good enough reason.

Ms. Strause also warns her clients to be prepared to have their personal lives exposed and examined, for any and all to see—especially when seeking a custody change or a modification in a visitation ruling. Character is the key issue in these cases. Anything can be asked about or exposed. The court can ask about the attitudes you've had about certain issues or ask questions regarding your personal life, sex life, and criminal history. Any question asked must be answered. For instance, a client may question what relevance a conviction for public intoxication fifteen years ago has to today's case. Ms. Strause's answer is, "Character counts." The client will need to convince the court that he or she is a different person today from what he or she was back then. Parents entering litigation have the idea that they can simply go into court and get what they want without any intrusion into their personal lives—a common but serious misconception.

REGARDING CHILD SUPPORT

Another misunderstanding has to do with child support. The question of who can claim the child on their taxes is a mud hole many parents slip into. Some noncustodial parents think they can claim the child on their taxes by virtue of the fact that they pay child support. Not so. According to Ms. Strause, IRS rules state that a parent can only claim the child on their taxes if the child lived with them at least 50 percent of the year. The exception to this rule would be if the custodial parent signs a waiver allowing the other parent to have the exemption or if an agreement of some sort has taken place. It costs the custodial parent much more to have a child living in their home than the money received through child support.

I questioned Ms. Strause on how a parent might know if they can get a change in a child support ruling. She said the best thing to do is check your state's child-support laws. You can easily do this, without paying an attorney, by downloading your state's child-support guidelines online. Find your state Web site and click on the judiciary link, or go to your state's bar association. These guidelines show how child support is determined in your state, such as the percentage of increase or decrease in wages necessary to get a modification of support. Going online and getting this information first can save you a lot of time and attorney fees.

MEDIATION

Taking into consideration the multitude of domestic cases Ms. Strause has worked in her seventeen years of practice, I asked her to tell me what advice she would give to parents before they enter any kind of litigation with their ex-spouse. Ms. Strause said she would advise any parent to bite their tongue and take it as long as they can. The less legal upset there is, the less effect it will have on the children. She would discourage anyone from jumping into litigation unless the situation becomes intolerable or if it is already affecting the children in a way that requires a resolution.

For parents who can still talk to each other, Ms. Strause suggests a wonderful alternative to court: mediation. Mediation is a situation where you, your former spouse, and any significant others (such as stepparents) meet together with a trained mediator to work out a solution to child-related problems. Ms. Strause says she has seen mediation work in about 80 percent of the cases. Because of its success, mediation has gained popularity across the nation.

The mediator does not make the decisions for you. They try to create an atmosphere where decisions can be made jointly about what is most important to both parents—their children. Generally, the mediator will guide the discussions between the parents into areas where they can work through the problems. If the mediator senses tension between the parties, they will often move the parents into separate rooms and caucus back and forth, discussing the issues until an agreement is reached. The mediator can be, but isn't necessarily, an attorney. A mediator costs about what a good attorney costs per hour, but the benefit in terms of what a child must go through when his parents go to court is priceless.

LOVE'S MOTIVATION

Love certainly is a motivating factor, but it should not be the only factor when you are considering the big step of going to court to resolve child-related issues. Obviously, as a Christian, you have much more to consider before you hire an attorney than just love for your children. My prayer is that you and your spouse first take this burden to the Lord. Next, take my three-point test to answer honestly any questions regarding motive, means, and method. Then, regardless of your decision, release your child to God.

The Scripture I used at the beginning of this chapter encapsulates every point I have tried to make within these pages: "He stores up sound wisdom for the upright; He is a shield to those who walk in integrity, guarding the paths of justice, and He preserves the way of His godly ones" (Prov. 2:7–8). What better promise than to know that if we put God first in our lives and walk in integrity, he will not only be our shield but he will give us wisdom to make the right choices. Think about it. We must trust God with our children— even if it means trudging through the muddy path of litigation. In the end, God will guard our path of justice and preserve our way.

Chapter Twelve

The Three Rs of Child Rearing: Teaching Children Character Values

Train up a child in the way he should go,
Even when he is old he will not depart from it.
~ Proverbs 22:6

Balancing the phone under my chin, I was up to my elbows in suds and dirty dishes. My mother-in-law was giving me chicken-frying instructions for the sixteenth time. For some reason, mine was always raw in the middle and burnt on the outside. In a constant effort to get my attention, Jeremy was throwing his toys onto the floor. I guess he was getting restless in his playpen. Who knows what actually prompted it? Maybe it was my total lack of concern or just his brilliant young mind. I don't know—but that's when it happened. My son looked right at me, reached out his pudgy little arms, and said, "Ma-ma."

I almost dropped the phone as I screamed to my mother-in-law, "Did you hear that?! Jeremy said 'ma-ma'! Can you believe it?" My mother-in-law and I screamed at Jeremy in unison, "Say it again! Say it again! Ma-ma, ma-ma!" Of course, after all the commotion he wasn't about to repeat the word, but it didn't matter—my son could talk!

My children's first words were so precious to me. The jubilant emotions I felt the day my firstborn son looked at me and said "ma-ma" drove me to call everyone I knew to report his remarkable genius. This incredible jubilance, however, was quickly sedated as my brilliant child expanded his vocabulary to include words like "no" and "mine."

The somber reality every parent faces in a child's life is the responsibility of teaching their children right from wrong. As Christians, we are given a charge by God to train up our children in the way they should go so that when they are old they will not depart from it (see Prov. 22:6). There is no greater reward for any parent than to see their children making good choices based on the standards they set for them—standards derived from God's Word. Few things compare in value to these treasures of a mother's or father's heart.

My mom taught me right from wrong in a lot of practical ways. Every mom has her "sayings"—clichés that were meant to drive home an instructional point. I can still hear her voice: "Shut the door! You weren't born in a barn," or "Clean up this room; it looks like a tornado came through here." Mom scolded, "Make your bed; we don't have maid service," and of course, after asking for fifty cents: "Money doesn't grow on trees." How many of us were ready to box up our brussel sprouts and send them to Africa after our mom exclaimed, "Don't waste your food; children in Africa are starving!"

As embarrassing as it is to admit, I've heard myself repeat these very phrases to my own children. Actually, there is something creepy about hearing your mother's words—words you hated hearing—coming from your own lips.

Mothers mean well; they just want their children to grow up to be responsible adults. Making beds, cleaning bedrooms, and managing money are skills and habits that don't come naturally. They are taught—most often by mom's persistent words. She sows the seed; and hopefully, her children reap the benefit in their adulthood. The Bible is full of promises to us seed-sowing parents, but my favorite comes from Isaiah 55:11:

> So will My word be which goes forth from My mouth;
> It will not return to Me empty,
> Without accomplishing what I desire,
> And without succeeding in the matter for which
> I sent it.

THE THREE RS OF CHILD-REARING

Just as the three Rs of education—reading, 'riting, and 'rithmetic—give children a foundation for making it in the working world, the three Rs of child-rearing—reverence, respect, and responsibility—equip them with a biblical foundation for succeeding in life. A child who has learned reverence for God, respect for others, and responsibility will grow up to be a confident adult who interacts well with other people, carrying a sense of integrity into all he does. You won't find the three Rs of child-rearing in your children's school textbooks, but you will find them in God's manual for life—the Bible.

The first R involves teaching a child to have *reverence* for God. The first and greatest commandment is to love the Lord your God. He is holy, just, and absolutely worthy of our reverence and honor. Without the seed of reverence, we have no basis to set any kind of standard in our lives, and "right" and "wrong" shift with the wind or mood of the moment. We'll have no regard for anyone or anything but ourselves. If it feels good, do it—no matter who gets hurt. Anyone left to himself will not only self-destruct, but his destruction will have a devastating affect on everyone around him. Look at Cain (see Gen. 4:3–8). Cain had no reverence for God, and his self-centeredness led him to murder his brother, Abel. If we don't teach our children to have reverence for God, they will live self-centered, destructive lives.

The second R stands for *respect*. We teach our kids first to love God and then to love others. Love for others is demonstrated by showing them respect. Every man, woman, and child has value to God; therefore, they should have value to us. Jesus said the second most important commandment after loving God was to love our neighbor as ourselves. As we give respect and love to others, we are respected and loved by others. The golden rule in Luke 6:31 says, "Treat others the same way you want them to treat you." But let's not stop there—Jesus didn't. He went on to say in Luke 6:38, "By your standard of measure it will be measured to you in return." We get back what we give out.

The third R means *responsibility*. We teach our children responsibility by teaching them God's Word. The Bible is filled with examples of those who lived responsibly and of those who didn't. We know from reading the Bible that we will gain God's approval and prosper in our ways if we act responsibly by living our lives in obedience to God's Word (see Ps. 1:1–3). On the opposite side of the coin, God's Word is just as clear about the consequences of an irresponsible, disobedient life (see Ps. 1:4–6).

THE SEED

It is clear that we must sow the seed that will enable our children to reap the benefits of reverence, respect, and responsibility. But where do we get the seed to sow? Well, in Arkansas we have an old country saying: The apple don't fall far from the tree. You and I, my friend, are the fruit-bearing trees. Jesus said, "Every good tree bears good fruit, but the bad tree bears bad fruit" (Matt. 7:17). It's all in the seed from mama and papa tree. In nature, a seed is an exact copy of the fruit that produced it. "Grapes are not gathered from thorn bushes" (Matt. 7:16). The same goes for spiritual seed. Parents set the example for their children to follow—good or bad.

The main way we teach values to our kids is by being an example to follow. Our actions and attitudes speak much louder than our words. We are an open book to our children, a living illustration of our own beliefs. Living out what we say we believe is the most effective tool we have in conveying godly values to our kids. People can say what they want about us—and they will—but our children will believe what they see in our actions.

It's important that children see their parents praying and reading the Bible. This shows them that God is more to us than a thing we do on Sunday mornings. They see that God is truly our source for wisdom and guidance. Children, from toddler age to teenage, watch their parents. What we do reflects what we believe. If they see us reading God's Word and they hear us praying as though we "know" God, they will take our faith seriously as we teach them to trust God. If we teach them to read and pray but they never see us do it, our words have very little weight.

If we tell our children to take the high road and forgive those who wrong them but we speak angrily to or about someone else, how can we expect them to do what we don't do ourselves? What example of respect will our children follow if they overhear us on the phone saying bad things about someone else—especially about his or her dad or mom?

Are you walking in integrity? Does your child see in you a good example of responsibility? For instance, when the check-out clerk makes a mistake by giving you too much change, do you give it back or do you buy your son an ice cream to celebrate? If we as parents want to plant the seeds of reverence, respect, and responsibility into our children's hearts, then we must possess and demonstrate these qualities in our lives as well.

REVERENCE

Harvey and I wanted to start our family out on strong footing from the beginning by having a time for family devotions; however, we met with a certain measure of resistance when we tried to incorporate it into our daily routine. Devotions did eventually find a place in our family, but it took time. Isn't it strange how bad habits seem to become established almost immediately but good habits always take a lot longer to develop? The habit of having family devotions developed in stages over a period of time.

The obvious place to initiate and incorporate godly values in our homes is by teaching our children to have reverence for God. Reading the Bible to our children not only teaches them about God and his character, but it also familiarizes them with biblical examples of how he has worked in the lives of his people through the ages. These examples, together with prayer, are important ingredients in teaching our children that they can have a personal relationship with Jesus.

If going to church and making God the foundation of your home is new to your children or stepchildren, jumping right in with "The Bible says . . ." preceding every correction or instruction will likely be met with resistance or resentment. They will see us as beating them over the heads with our Bibles (figuratively speaking, of course) rather than demonstrating God's love. Of course, it's good for our children to see us read our Bibles and to have us show them how it applies to their lives in the way of correction, encouragement, and instruction, but there is a positive and a negative way to do this. Introducing biblical correction and instruction to a blended family often takes a delicate hand of balance.

My three children were familiar with daily devotions growing up—until my three-job work schedule as a single mom squeezed out the time for it. We prayed together at bedtime and meals, but family devotions disappeared from their daily lives. Because Harvey made his commitment to the Lord after he and his ex-wife were separated, his children had never been exposed to family devotions. After Harvey and I had been married two years, we received custody of the girls. Our family was again making major adjustments. Adjusting wasn't easy for any of us—for the parents, for the children who were used to living with us, or for those in the transitional state.

During any adjustment period, emotions tend to run higher than normal, especially in teenagers. Bearing this in mind, we began working toward establishing family devotions with sensitivity toward everyone in the family. We didn't gather as a family right away for devotions, but we started slowly with prayer. Like introducing new wine to old wineskins, we had to allow our family a little time for aging to prevent it from bursting (see Luke 5:37).

Every meal began with prayer, whether in our home or in a restaurant. By giving thanks to God for our meals, we taught our children to acknowledge God for the things we otherwise took for granted. We often included thanks for other things in our mealtime prayer, such as an A Sara made on a test, Mandi's recovery from a cold, or praise for a new friend our shy daughter, Jodie, made at school. We even added small requests, such as asking God to help Aaron with an upcoming algebra test or Jennifer in her basketball game. Although all mealtime prayers were simple and to the point, they brought our family closer together and demonstrated God's hand in our everyday lives. Most importantly, we were gathering before God as a family. I love the saying "A family that prays together, stays together" because our family did and has.

Once our family was established and we had time to "age," we decided to expand our daily prayer to an actual family devotional time. Doing this was easier said than done. Deciding *what* we would do and *when* to do it posed our biggest challenge. Evenings were taken up with all the preparations for the next school day, such as homework and baths, so we decided to have it in the mornings. Because the time we had in the mornings was limited, we had to find material that would fit into our schedule.

Our children's ages were also an important factor to consider. We found a juvenile devotional book that appealed to the girls, but the teenagers lost interest. If we tried to do something for the older children, the young ones were lost. We tried several different family devotional books but finally decided the best thing to do was just to read directly from the Scriptures.

It was easier for me to choose books of the Bible and read short portions of Scripture, taking a small bite each day, depending on how full our morning was. Our family would then discuss the reading and how it applied to us. Discussions were on each child's level. After we read and discussed the Scripture, we closed in prayer. Most days our family devotions lasted twenty to thirty minutes. Some of our shortest readings held the best discussions and carried the greatest impact. The one that immediately comes to mind is from 1 Corinthians 15:33: "Bad company corrupts good morals." What child or teenager doesn't have to make choices about who their friends will be? This short verse enabled us to discuss *why* they should choose friends wisely.

Every family is different with its own routine. There are no set rules for how, when, or how long your family time should be. We had more time for longer devotions in the summer. For convenience sake, we moved our devotions to later in the afternoon so the kids could sleep late. When the kids were in school and we were rushed for time, we just read a verse and prayed together as a family. Family devotions don't have to be an hour long to have their desired effect. They do, however, have to be consistent and sincere—reflective of the parent's faith.

Our children learned to reverence God by seeing his compassionate character every day in his Word during devotions. By beginning slowly with prayer, we were able to teach our kids to look to God in the daily circumstances of their lives. We prayed over the big things as well as the small incidental things. These prayers taught our kids to look beyond their own limited wisdom and abilities to a loving, caring God who has their best interest in the forefront of his mind. They were then able to make the natural progression into a daily reading of God's Word and praying together as a family.

Stories like David and Goliath taught our kids that trusting in a big God is wiser than trusting in a big spear. By giving them biblical examples to follow, our kids were equipped with the weapons they would need for approaching difficult circumstances. During the turbulent years of blending our family, the truths learned in our morning devotions became the bedrock of faith for everyone in the house—whether they realized it or not. Sure, our kids rolled their eyes, moaned, and groaned when we called them to morning devotions; but I firmly believe the seeds of reverence sown into their lives have born fruit.

RESPECT

Prayer and Bible reading are good places to begin teaching children reverence for God; but as any parent will testify, it is only the beginning. A house with kids offers plenty of opportunities to apply the second R of child-rearing: *respect*. The Word of God is the best guide for teaching our children to be respectful to others.

David again is a great biblical example. In the book of 1 Samuel, you can read how King Saul tried to kill David. David wasn't Saul's enemy; in fact, David was his faithful son-in-law and the best warrior in his army. But Saul relentlessly hunted David down, doing everything in his power to destroy him. Why? Because of Saul's jealousy. If anyone ever had good reason to disrespect someone, David had more than enough with King Saul.

On one occasion David had opportunity to destroy King Saul while he slept in a cave. David and one of his men crept quietly into the cave with the purpose of killing the king. After seeing the sleeping king, the soldier begged David to let him kill the king with one swift motion of his spear, but David could do Saul no harm. Why? Respect. This is a difficult concept for some of us to understand unless we recognize where David's respect was directed. Look at David's words: "Do not destroy him, for who can stretch out his hand against the LORD's anointed and be without guilt?" (1 Sam. 26:9). David's respect wasn't directed at Saul; it was directed at God.

David had a deep reverence for God, and because of this reverence, he respected God's anointed—King Saul. David knew Saul was an evil man. He also knew that Saul would never extend the same kind of mercy to him if the roles were reversed. Out of respect for God, however, David took the high road and left the king alone.

You might be thinking, *So what does that have to do with me?* Do you have a King Saul in your life, someone who is a constant aggravation, an itch that won't go away? Maybe your Saul is as bad as David's. Parents can learn from biblical examples as well as children. Maybe your Saul isn't an anointed king; it doesn't matter, because Jesus instructs us to respect them anyway. Luke 6:27–28 reads, "But I say to you who hear, love your enemies, do good to those who hate you, bless those who curse you, pray for those who mistreat you." This, of course, is a very hard saying, especially when you have to deal with difficult people and circumstances in your life.

The message David was trying to convey to his soldier was this: "God will take care of this guy, but I don't want my disrespect for God to cost me or any of my men the kingdom." We can say the same thing: "God will take care of this person, but I don't want my disrespect for God to cost me my children or my family."

David let the king sleep and left the cave without harming him. He took only the king's javelin and water jug. After reaching a safe distance from the king's army, David called out and woke them up. He displayed the javelin and water jug, demonstrating to everyone that even though he had the chance to destroy his enemy, he chose mercy. When we choose to overlook other people's words and actions against us, we are doing the same thing. Remember, our children learn more from our actions than from our words.

Choose to take the high road and demonstrate mercy by your words and actions. Even if the person in question is your ex, God will reveal the truth in the end. As Scripture tells us in Proverbs 22:6, if your child, by your example, learns how to respect others while they are young, then when they are adults, they will know how to live and work in this world in a way that is pleasing to God.

Respectfully dealing with difficult people is one way of teaching our children, but there are many other ways we can incorporate respect into their daily lives. By teaching our kids common courtesies, they will learn to think of others as well as themselves. The following list gives a few examples you might implement in and around your home and family:

- Knock before opening a closed door.

- Ask if anyone would like to share the last of the mashed potatoes before you scoop them up for yourself.

- Open the door for your stepsister if you see she has her hands full.

- Fold the clothes that were left in the dryer by someone else instead of stuffing them into a basket to get wrinkled.

- Hang up your towel after you take a shower instead of leaving it for someone else to pick up.

- Ask your stepbrother standing next to you if he wants you to make him a sandwich while you're making one for yourself.

Treating other people the way we want to be treated is commonly known as the golden rule (see Luke 6:31). In blended families, a wall of division between "my family" and "your family" exists for the first year or two. Seeing past this division is especially hard for children. They must be taught in practical, everyday ways to reach beyond their own little world to a step-sibling or stepparent. Respect must be taught in the little things before it can be accepted in the big things, but it is only the first step in developing good character values in our children. The next step is right on its heels.

RESPONSIBILITY

Character-building values such as integrity, honesty, work ethics, stewardship, and patience are developed through the third R of child rearing: *responsibility.* This character value is a vital part of your child's training because it will shape how your child conducts his affairs as an adult.

BEING ANSWERABLE

Responsibility, by Webster's definition, is a noun: "the state of being answerable." Teaching a child responsibility is to teach them to be answerable for whatever they say or do. If a child knows he must give an account for his actions, words, or deeds, he will strive to do them well. On the opposite side of the coin, however, if a child is not taught responsibility, he will show little concern for the job he does—if he does the job at all. He has no one to answer to.

Children learn responsibility in a number of different ways, but Harvey and I found that a reward system worked best for our family. As early as four or five years old, our kids began asking for money. Much as we wanted to give our children good things, we had to set some boundaries—not just because our paychecks were limited but because it was our responsibility to teach our children that they can't have anything and everything they want just because they ask for it. Distinguishing between *needs* and *wants* seems to come easier if the child is spending his or her own earnings to get it. We hoped that they would value items more if they spent their own money on them—maybe even enough to take care of them.

THE CLARK SYSTEM

"Mom, can I have a couple of dollars to go to the store with my friends?" "Dad, will you buy me this CD?" Sound familiar? Multiply this request by five or six wanting children, and then divide the sum by one severely stretched paycheck. The answer is a very difficult math problem for many blended families with several kids to feed and care for.

My husband, being an entrepreneur with a keen understanding of profit and loss, came up with a plan not only to teach our children the value of a dollar but also to instill character building values into their lives. The "Clark System" took the institution of "allowances" to a whole new level. It even had its own currency—Clark dollars and Clark quarters.

Keeping up with all of the household tasks kept me pretty busy, but Harvey and I wanted the kids to do some of the work as well. We tried to teach them responsibility by having them carry part of the load. We wanted them to share in the household chores because they lived in the house and were part of the family. They did not receive an allowance for keeping their rooms in order or if we asked them to pick up their "campsite" in front of the TV. But kids do seem always to need a little spending money. This need prompted Harvey and me to come up with the means for them to earn an allowance/spending money.

Harvey's plan was actually pretty simple. If the kids did their assigned jobs, they were paid according to the value of the job. Some were worth more than others. If they didn't do the job, they didn't get paid. In addition to the jobs, there were fines for breaking household rules. Some offenses cost more than others. If they broke the rules, they paid the price—in Clark dollars. Not wanting to emphasize the negative, we also incorporated bonuses and rewards into the system. If one of the kids was especially courteous or went the extra mile, they were rewarded in, what else? Clark dollars, of course.

Clark quarters were round, black, quarter-sized disks with holes punched out of the center, while Clark dollars were about the size of a silver dollar. Harvey die cut both from material scraps in his shop. When we went to town and the kids needed spending money, they could redeem their Clark currency for the real thing.

In addition to teaching our children to save, tithe, and respect one another's property, our children also learned to be responsible for their own money. At the end of each week, they would receive their "pay." This plan worked pretty well for us. We were actually able to stay on top of a lot of the little chores that can pile up in a busy household, such as emptying the trash cans and clearing off the catch-all counter in the kitchen.

The flip side of paying our children money for chores is that they didn't always understand the value of money. They tended to leave money lying around the house for someone else to come along and claim. Fights over claimed quarters and dollars sprang up continuously. Harvey and I didn't want to "throw the baby out with the bath water" by eliminating allowances all together, but there had to be a way to teach the kids good -steward--ship. My answer was to give every child in the Clark home a place to keep their earnings—a money bag.

I made small, red drawstring bags with the first initial of each child's name sewn on it. The red bags held only Clark currency. Each child was responsible for putting his or her money in their own bag. If Clark money was found lying around the house, it was their loss. Stray money went back into the Clark bank. The prospect of losing their hard-earned "cash" promoted a greater measure of responsibility in all the kids. The loose "change" found its way into the proper bags in no time at all.

Instead of giving the kids a free allowance each week, they learned to work for their money. They also learned that if they didn't work, they didn't get paid. Their negligence was felt later when they wanted to go to a movie with their friends and their money bag was empty. Our house was kept in better order because the chores were shared by everyone in the house instead of the bulk of the work falling on me.

Because of the "Clark system," the kids were more aware of their manners and had more respect for other people's property without my having to nag them. I think our kids appreciated having black-and-white guidelines generically set up for everyone in the house. No one was pointed out or picked on for breaking the rules; they were simply corrected by losing a Clark quarter. Taking advantage of this system, we also hoped to break some of the children's bad habits—like rocking back in my kitchen chairs.

Our kids had this particularly annoying habit of rocking back in my ladder-back kitchen chairs during dinner. Unfortunately, the chairs were easily broken where the back is joined to the seat. The added pressure and weight from rocking backward ruined more than one of my kitchen chairs. This offense cost the offender a Clark quarter every time he or she rocked backwards.

This penalty worked well for a time, until my son Aaron, a testy teenager who was especially bad about rocking the chairs, rocked back during dinner. I said to him, "Aaron, that's a quarter." He grumbled a little, but then a few minutes later, accidentally did it again. Annoyed at his continual rocking, I said, "Another quarter, Aaron."

Aaron scanned the faces of everyone around the table watching him, then looked directly at me and smiled. With both hands, he grabbed the table and rocked back and forth five or six more times while simultaneously chiming out, "Cha-ching! Cha-ching! Cha-ching!" The whole table broke out in laughter, forever ending the quarter penalty for chair-rocking. It was nice while it lasted, but I was never again able to charge a quarter for the offense because the offender would always pull Aaron's "cha-ching!" stunt. "Cha-ching!" became our family joke.

We actually had a lot of fun with the Clark dollars. Good-natured play and laughter is a healing medicine for any blended family. We can't take ourselves so seriously in our efforts to break bad habits that we end up breaking a child's spirit. Our Clark System taught our children the value of responsibility, integrity, and the value of a dollar, while allowing them room to adapt to and enjoy their new family.

From babbling babes to trying teens and all the way into adulthood, our children are our greatest treasure on earth. Sowing reverence, respect, and responsibility into their lives takes time. It may seem as if we are throwing a lot of seed to the wind, but if we are diligent and consistent in our efforts to sow into prepared ground and water it with prayer, the good seed of God's Word will take root in their lives and produce a godly -harvest.

Chapter Thirteen

Joining Two Households

What therefore God has joined together,
let no man separate.
~ Mark 10:9

Sitting across the table from each other, Harvey and I surveyed the pile of papers in front of us. Along with child support and other household bills, we had two JCPenney cards, two Sears cards, two MasterCards, two house payments, two car payments, two sets of utility bills, and two empty bank accounts. Feeling the weight, we put our two heads together, hoping to keep our necks above the water. If God could keep Noah afloat in the ark after all the animals entered two by two, surely he could keep our house afloat when we joined our bills two by two. Just as with Noah, we didn't have a clue about what we were doing. Noah, Harvey, and I simply obeyed God, followed a plan, and God made it float.

Like most remarried couples, Harvey and I discovered a colorful new dimension to the following passage of Scripture: "And the two shall become one" (Mark 10:8). Merging two established households is much more involved than blending parents and their kids (though that is hard enough)—it's blending everything from lifestyles, incomes, and debts to houses, furniture, and pets. Becoming "one" involves determining where to live and which schools the kids should attend, as well as sorting through all the stuff the two families have accumulated over the years. What *do* you do with four TVs, three VCRs, two microwaves, and an extra washer and dryer? It didn't take long for us to feel as overwhelmed as the old woman in the shoe, who had so many children (and TVs), she didn't know what to do.

Overwhelming as it might be, figuring out schools, sleeping arrangements, and sorting through multiple appliances is actually the easy part of tying our family knots. The arduous part of blending remains stretching paychecks over an inflated household without snapping.

I'll never forget the pressure Harvey and I felt the day we got custody of his daughters. Because of the circumstances surrounding the custody change, we did not have any school clothes for them. We had no choice but to make a trip to the mall and buy three new wardrobes. This was great for the girls, but it was a real financial strain on Harvey and me. All we had was a JCPenney card nearing the maximum limit.

My stair-"step" daughters were close in size, so we bought a whole stack of inexpensive T-shirts in every color. Thankfully, the layered look (taking two T-shirts and rolling up the sleeves to expose the bottom shirt color) was really in. This multiplied the color options for all three girls, and with a variety of matching pants, we had a suitable, cheap solution to the clothing dilemma.

It would have been nice to have a brand-new beginning financially, like when we were young adults starting out on our own; but unfortunately, blended families usually don't have that luxury. We might be getting a fresh new start with the man or woman of our dreams; but our ways of handling money, as well as our debts, credit histories, and lifestyles, are already established.

Romantic thoughts of riding off into the sunset with our wonderful new mate are interrupted by the reality of bringing two households into one. Once the honeymoon is over, lovebirds return to their nest—where mom's kids inform her of their need for new shoes, and dad's kids remind him they're out of school supplies and lunch money. When we get home, it's life as usual—times two.

JOINING HEARTS

Like every other dream newlywed couples have of their marriage, building a new life together financially requires a joining of hearts—first with God and then with each other. Our combined faith armors us for the battles we encounter on a daily basis, including those related to money (see Matt. 18:19–20). God wants us to join our hearts with his—to live, manage, and enjoy an abundant life by applying the truth of his Word to every financial challenge we face as a family. However, joining hearts over credit card bills and bank statements doesn't put one in a very romantic or Christlike mood.

A newlywed couple stepping into the quandaries of blending their family finances may feel that they're venturing into a minefield. Walking through sensitive, emotional topics such as money, debt, and debt management is difficult enough, but dodging disagreements in family goals and the means to accomplish them can turn a simple purchase into a marital explosion.

Money touches every part of our lives: the food we eat, the house we live in, our jobs, our entertainment, our retirement, our kids' education, our self-esteem, and even our relationship with God. If we aren't in unity with each other and with God about money, we will only find confusion. The financial pressures of combining two households or just dealing with unexpected surprises (such as our clothing dilemma) can set us up for disaster.

A good first step toward disarming these potentially explosive land mines is for you and your spouse to sit down together and do the following:

1. Join your hearts together in prayer.

2. Honestly evaluate your financial situation.

3. Discuss realistic expectations of each other.

4. Come to an agreement on your family's financial goals.

5. Decide together how to reach those goals.

6. Make a commitment to each other and to God to follow through with your plan.

Even finding the time and having the energy to talk about finances can be difficult. You may want to do this at the first of the month, after you've gotten all your bills together. Choose a time of day when nothing else is on your mind to distract you: the kids are in bed, both parties are in a good mood, the dishes are done, and the TV is turned off. Begin with prayer.

As a couple in Christ, we are accountable to God and each other for every decision we make. If we do not join our hearts over budgets and expenditures, how can we join our hearts over other family goals?

What God Has Joined, Let No Man Separate

Marriage consists of a covenant between a man and a woman. How the two become one remains one of God's mysteries. God said in Mark 10:9: "What therefore God has joined together, let no man separate." Our commitment to join body and soul includes our finances as well. A husband and wife, regardless of their past, cannot become one if they separate incomes and debts into "his money" and "her money."

Everything belongs to God. All money and possessions have been entrusted to both of you. Keeping finances separated sows a seed of division, and the Bible says that a house divided against itself cannot stand (see Matt. 12:25). (Of course, college funds or inheritances for children from previous marriages should be addressed prayerfully, with clear, open communication between husband and wife. Talk to a financial counselor or an attorney to set up a will or trust to address these matters. You also should discuss any issues of child support or alimony and how it should be used.)

Separating finances refers to keeping your paychecks and bills within the "mine" and "theirs" categories. For example, if a husband lays claim to his paycheck with certain bills that he brought into the marriage, and a wife claims her paycheck and the household bills, there exists a formula for division. If the husband pays all of his bills and has money left over, he probably feels no remorse about buying himself a new car stereo. His wife, however, is scraping by with her check, barely covering the household expenses because the electric bill was high that month. Hubby is enjoying his new tunes while his wife is trying to figure out how to make it until next payday.

Resentments build quickly in this scenario because husband and wife have not joined their hearts with God's, giving him ownership of their possessions. If a couple truly wants to become one and tie their family knot for life, they must relinquish ownership of their finances. Remember, our hearts are linked to our treasures. If we want to join our hearts together, we must join our treasures as well.

Joining our treasures also includes joining our debts. Marriage is a lifelong commitment, and it no longer matters who actually put their name on the dotted line or when. As a husband and wife enter the covenant of marriage, they vow to love one another for better or worse, for richer or poorer, until death do they part. Their debt becomes your debt, just as their treasures become yours. If, for instance, a husband has bad credit because of his ex-wife's misdeeds, the new wife must absorb this "for worse" into the joining of hearts. However, because you've both joined hearts with God, he will give you the wisdom necessary to arrive at the "for better" stage of your marriage.

The same principle applies to child support. I've heard women complain about having to pay their husband's ex-wife child support. The moment you entered into the marriage covenant, his children became yours, and yours his. Don't look at it as "paying" the ex; look at it as "supporting" his child. You'll find the pill a little easier to swallow.

UNLIKELY MONOPOLY PARTNERS

Because men and women tend to view their finances through different lenses, their eyes must be on God for clear direction. Of course, we are all different, but generally, women tend to cling to a secure job and steady income like a warm security blanket, while men equate their own worth and value with the ability to conquer financial challenges and provide for their family's needs. One of the biggest challenges to joining our hearts financially is our naturally different hearts.

As Harvey and I sat down together with all of the bills, we made a remarkable discovery—Harvey and I had very different ideas about money, debt, goals, and financial planning.

Harvey is a businessman. He manages his business and finances the same way he plays Monopoly. He says he can tell a lot about people by playing a game of Monopoly with them. His strategy is to observe how his opponents meet opportunities and challenges. Harvey looks to see if they are risk takers or if they hold tightly to their possessions. With the observations he makes after only a few times around the board, Harvey is able to use his opponents' strengths and weaknesses to his advantage.

Once he has a clear understanding of the whole board and all the players, he likes to take risks. No one in our family ever wants to play Monopoly with Harvey because he usually wins. "Wins" is putting it mildly. A more apt description would be, he unmercifully wallops them. As they are sent off to the poorhouse to mortgage everything they own to pay him rent, they inevitably come up short and are kicked out of the game in humility.

I, on the other hand, have a background in banking. When we play Monopoly, I'm always the banker. Before I married Harvey, I worked in the lending department of a bank and in a mortgage company. I am very black-and-white when it comes to finances. I look at all the checks and balances before making a decision. If I had a Monopoly motto, it would be "play it safe." I like the security of a savings account and a low debt-to-income ratio. Taking financial risks is not in my nature. Needless to say, Harvey and I don't make very good Monopoly game partners.

We are worlds apart on our financial philosophies, but somehow God has brought us together to establish our financial goals. We came together because we both wanted what was best for our family. Harvey had to give a little to meet my need for security, and I had to give a little to allow him to build up the business for our family's future. As in every other area of our marriage, communication and trust were key elements in our compromise. We discussed every financial decision because both of us had the same objective in mind—the good of our family.

Before we married, Harvey didn't have any particular system for paying his bills or keeping up with his billing statements. He had paperwork and receipts scattered everywhere. I found them in his truck, his office, and the house. In Harvey's eyes, designing reproduction parts from the samples he pulled from old cars in the junkyard was a much better use of his time than balancing a checkbook. In fact, Harvey never really concerned himself too much with balancing the checkbook; he just kept enough money in the account to stay ahead of the checks. In our home, the question "Who should do the bookkeeping?" never came up. My banking experience and need for order made me the obvious choice.

As long as a husband and wife communicate and eventually agree on their financial decisions, it doesn't matter who actually writes the checks or puts the statements away. If I expected Harvey to do this job because he is the man of the house, both of our stress levels would be elevated. He would hate it because it doesn't come naturally, and I would hate it because nothing would be in order.

I have found that it is always best to operate within your God-given gifts and abilities. If the husband is better with financial organization than his wife, he should take on the job. The important things are open communication, agreement on financial decisions affecting the family, and the management of your finances with a system that works for you. Our natural differences as a husband and wife will complement each other as we join hearts to achieve our common goal—the good of our family.

ALIGNING FINANCIAL GOALS WITH SPIRITUAL VALUES

By aligning our financial goals with our spiritual values, we are digging another shovel of dirt toward the solid "Rock" foundation.

To do this, we must lay our finances, alongside our bodies, on the altar as a sacrifice to God (see Rom. 12:1). Once a sacrifice is offered to God, it cannot be taken back; it no longer belongs to us. It is holy—set apart for God's use.

The late Larry Burkett, founder and chairman of the board of Crown Financial Ministries, once wrote, "The way we behave is a surefire indicator of what we truly believe."[1] In his article "Belief and Behavior," Mr. Burkett said, "When Christian people really start to *'believe'* what the Bible teaches about money—that is, when their financial behavior actually begins to conform to Scripture— we'll see a radical change in the effectiveness and vitality of the church."[2]

Acting out what we believe also radically affects our marriages and homes. I consulted with Richard and Todd Sadowski, a father-son counseling team from Christian Financial Principles, for expert advice on financial management. Christian Financial Principles is an organization of financial counselors who have surrendered their business to Christ with the purpose of helping people align their financial goals with spiritual values.

Too often we want to keep our money separate from our faith, but Todd Sadowski says, "How people handle their money is a good barometer of where they are spiritually." He added, "If you open a person's checkbook, you can see what is important. Just as Jesus said, 'For where your treasure is, there your heart will be also' (Luke 12:34)."

As Christians, we need to ask ourselves, "What do I believe about money?" The Bible tells us in 1 Chronicles 29:11 and in Psalm 24:1 that God owns everything, but do we believe it? Open your checkbook and take a look. How does your barometer read? Is there a storm brewing?

Todd and Richard Sadowski believe many Christians today do not have a complete understanding of their responsibility for good financial stewardship because the world has interfered with the truth of God's Word. The world tells us that happiness and fulfillment come from money. Even Christians have slowly bought into the idea that the money we earn and the possessions we hold belong to us, not to God.

Understanding our role as "steward" of the money and possessions with which we are entrusted comes easier if we truly believe that everything belongs to God. A steward is someone with the responsibility of overseeing his master's belongings, treating them as if they were his own. *Webster's Dictionary* defines *stewardship* as "the careful and responsible management of something entrusted to one's care." A Christian man or woman with a stewardship mentality toward finances understands accountability to God.

Accountability, of course, means there will be a day of judgment when we stand before God and give account for the money and possessions that were under our control while we lived on this earth. If we have done well as stewards, we will be rewarded. If we have acted foolishly, our works will burn up (see 1 Cor. 3:13–15).

Accountability to God is ongoing. As we follow God's principles of sowing and reaping, we harvest a crop—reaping a reward not only here on the earth but also in eternity. If we choose to be lazy or to squander our money, we will enter heaven without a reward. As we show ourselves faithful with our money, by making wise choices and sowing into the kingdom of God, we will be blessed with more. The better we manage the finances entrusted to us, the more we will be entrusted with.

"He who is faithful in a very little thing is faithful also in much; and he who is unrighteous in a very little thing is unrighteous also in much. Therefore if you have not been faithful in the use of unrighteous wealth, who will entrust the true riches to you?" (Luke 16:10–12)

BUDGETING

Having a plan of action—a budget with goals—is extremely important for blending two families into one. Todd Sadowski says, "If you fail to plan, you are planning to fail." Proverbs 29:18 puts it another way: "Where there is no vision, the people are unrestrained." Without a goal or vision to direct their actions, they do as they please, with no purpose for the future.

Without a plan you will find it extremely difficult to reach any financial goals, so I asked Todd to give couples who are struggling with blending their finances some general advice. He encourages couples to

- develop a workable budget,

- get out of debt,

- save cash, and

- start investing for the long run—college education fund, retirement, future goals, and charitable outreaches.

If you are having trouble coming up with a workable budget, the Sadowskis advise you to seek help through a professional Christian financial service, such as Christian Financial Principles. However, financial counseling isn't limited to professionals. Local churches often offer this service, or a friend who is financially stable may be willing to work with you.

The important thing is to have a plan in place so that you can reach the goal of making more money than you spend every month. Once you meet this goal, you can begin working toward more long-term financial goals for your family's future.

Christian Financial Principles recommends a budget plan as a guideline for those who need a general idea of how to break down their income and debt into a budget form. Todd and Richard stress, however, there are no cookie-cutter solutions to planning out a budget and family financial goals. Every family is different with different needs. The Sadowskis advise following Crown Financial Ministries' general budgeting guideline.³ Use it as a compass to guide you in planning your family budget.

GENERAL BUDGET GUIDELINES

You should plan out a livable budget to meet your financial obligations with your "net" income. Your "gross" income is the total amount of income before taxes and your 10 percent tithe are deducted. What is left is considered your "net" income. From your net income, use the following percentages to budget your household expenses:

32%	Housing
13%	Food
13%	Auto
5%	Debts
5%	Insurance
6%	Recreation/Entertainment
5%	Clothing
4%	Medical/Dental
5%	Savings
5%	School/Childcare
5%	Investments
7%	Miscellaneous

After Harvey and I combined our income and totaled all of our bills, child support, and household expenses, we had to come up with some sort of a plan to pay everything. We prayed about it together and then worked out a budget we could live with. Our budgets have changed over the years as our circumstances have changed. When Harvey and I married, we had three children living at home and three children living with their mother. A year later we had five children living at home and one adult child living on his own. Our budget adjusted with the addition of Jodie's braces and Aaron's art lessons. Every time a child went to the prom, graduated, or moved out of the house, our finances changed. My point is this: be flexible, and build a cushion into your budget for emergencies.

TITHING

The tithe is the "firstfruits" of your labor—the first 10 percent. In Malachi 2:7–3:12, God tells his people to return to him. When they ask him how to return, he responds by telling them to bring the whole tithe into his storehouse, even going so far as to accuse them of robbing him. God doesn't need our money. He owns the cattle on a thousand hills—he even owns the hills. God is looking for men and women who will give him their heart. Again, our treasures are linked to our heart, and by bringing God *his tithe,* we are in turn bringing God our heart.

Obedience in the tithe when you're broke may seem like foolishness at first glance; but on closer examination of God's Word, we see benefits that far outnumber the sacrifice. Malachi 3:10 is the only command God gives with a challenge to test him: "'Test Me now in this,' says the LORD of hosts, 'if I will not open for you the windows of heaven and pour out for you a blessing until it overflows.'" If this is not enough motivation for us to tithe, God goes on with yet another incentive in the two verses that follow: "'Then I will rebuke the devourer for you, so that it will not destroy the fruits of the ground; nor will your vine in the field cast its grapes,' says the LORD of hosts." God is not only promising to pour out overflowing blessings, but he also will keep the enemy from devouring what we do have. When God says our vine in the field will not cast its grapes, he is assuring us that our work will not be in vain.

If we are obedient by giving God the tithe, he will give us so many blessings that we won't be able to contain them. He'll make our work fruitful so that others will recognize it and call us blessed (see Mal. 3:12). On the other hand, if we aren't obedient in the tithe, there is a curse (see Mal. 3:9). When we aren't tithing, we are leaving ourselves open and vulnerable to the devourer. In 1 Peter 5:8, God tells us to be on the alert because "your adversary, the devil, prowls around like a roaring lion, seeking someone to devour."

Richard and Todd told me a story about an aunt in their family who was always faithful to the tithe, even when it made no sense financially to do so. At a time when she was barely scraping by and didn't have enough money to pay both her $32.18 gas bill and her tithe, she chose to tithe. The very next day she received an unexpected refund check in the mail from the electric company for exactly $32.18—the very amount she needed to pay her gas bill.

The Sadowskis' aunt is just one in a sea of testimonies. I could write another book of stories people have shared telling how God proved himself over and over again when they were faithful to put God first and pay their tithes.

Richard Sadowski sums up the tithe in this way: "The tithe is an act of worship. God doesn't need a penny of our money. He wants what is in our hearts—a showing of our faith and trust in him."

MARSHMALLOWS AND SPIDERS

I asked Richard and Todd Sadowski what they saw to be the biggest problem for remarried couples who came to Christian

Financial Principles for counseling. Without hesitation they said it was debt.

Todd told me of a psychological study done with small children and marshmallows. Several children were offered a choice. They could have either two marshmallows today or one today and two tomorrow. Most of the children chose the instant gratification of two today, even though they knew they would get more marshmallows if they waited. Todd says American adults have the same mentality as those children. They do not want to wait and get what is best for them tomorrow. Debt gives people the ability to get what they want right now. They know it's not good for them, but to have that instant gratification, they do it anyway.

Todd explained further, "If someone had a fear of spiders, and you brought them step by step, day by day, closer and closer to spiders, they would overcome their fear because of the systematic desensitization." In similar fashion we have experienced a systematic desensitization to debt in America. At one time in this country, debt was a bad thing; but slowly, over the years, debt has crept into our lives through a combination of systematic desensitization and the desire for instant gratification.

Todd says we need first to know the difference between *needs, wants,* and *desires.* He defined the differences like this: we *need* transportation to work, we *want* a new car, and we *desire* a Mercedes. Until we are on track with our goals, we should cut back on our wants and desires. In other words, stop using your credit cards! Call each of the companies to cancel the cards, get out a sharp pair of scissors, and cut them up. Before spending money on wants and desires, we need to understand why we are in debt and then do all we can to pay off those debts.

Prioritizing your debts into categories is a good way to approach debt reduction. Christian Financial Principles recommends concentrating on the highest interest rate debts first, even before saving for your long-term goals. The interest you earn on a savings account will be less than what you are paying out on debt.

BRINGING DOWN THE GIANT

Getting defensive and angry with those we love is a natural response to financial pressures; but as we develop a relationship with God in prayer, he clothes us in his protective armor. Thoughts entering our minds telling us to give up or to war against our spouse, our creditors, or our ex are repelled by our shield of faith because our confidence is in God rather than ourselves or someone else.

Time spent with God in prayer makes us even stronger as we feed ourselves on his Word, the Bible. As food nourishes the physical body, so the Word of God nourishes our spiritual body. God's Word arms us with the weapons we need to do battle. As we get to know God and his character, we begin to see our financial circumstances from a steward's perspective.

Consider David for a moment. David chose to put all of his confidence and trust in God. He lived a life of faith and obedience. When Goliath challenged the army of Israel and taunted their God, David took offense (see 1 Sam. 17). He didn't see a nine-foot giant who had been a warrior from his youth. David saw a foolish Philistine man who placed his faith in his stature, his heavy armor, and his javelin. He didn't see Goliath as a threat because David believed in God. He knew God was bigger.

Though David's resolve landed him in a face-to-face confrontation with the Philistine army and a giant who towered over him, he knew God stood beside him, ready to fight for what belonged to God. We can have that same resolve when facing our creditors and our combined household bills. When we place our confidence in God, we are obediently placing our small stone in the sling, trusting God to bring down the giant.

Remember, everything belongs to God, and we are simply his stewards. He will fight for us. Facing a pile of bills with a limited income may look and feel to us as if we are up against a nine-foot giant—armed with only a small stone in a sling. If, however, we've prepared ourselves spiritually by joining our hearts, we will have a whole new perspective on the battle. Instead of looking to our limited resources to bring down the giant, we will be looking to the God of the universe. The giant will suddenly weaken and wither once we realize, "Hey, God is on my side!"

Chapter Fourteen

LOAVES AND FISHES: MAKING USE OF EVERY REMNANT

But all things must be done properly
and in an orderly manner.
~ 1 Corinthians 14:40

*Y*ou give them something to eat!" This was Jesus' response to the
disciples when they asked him to send the multitude away for
dinner. They'd been outside all day listening to a sermon, probably
standing, as hour after hour passed with nothing to eat. Not only
had they been doing this, but all those people were probably still
standing there at the end of the sermon, with simultaneously
growling stomachs, wondering what's next. Can you imagine the
sea of kids tugging on their mothers' tunics crying, "Mom, I'm
hungry"? How were the disciples going to pull this one off? Having
walked a mile or two in their sandals, I know just how the poor
guys must have felt when they had to come up with enough food

to feed thousands. Of course, my multitude was on a smaller scale, but for me and my husband, it was just as intimidating.

Harvey and I brought our family together under the condition of very tight quarters—not the kind of quarters you live in, but the kind you grip tightly as you walk the aisles of the -supermarket. Some accused me of being so tight they could hear me squeak when I walked. The financial pressures of blending a family can be as overwhelming as trying to feed the multitudes with only a basketful of loaves and fishes.

The Bible says that there were five thousand men. When you add the women and children, the number was probably closer to fifteen thousand. That's enough people to fill a good-sized arena—without concession stands! Can't you just see the disciples scrambling around trying to find food to feed all those people? They tried to meet the impossible situation as any of us would—with normal, practical solutions. Remembering the time Jesus miraculously filled their fishing nets, Peter and Andrew were probably thinking about putting their boat out for another big catch; possibly others checked their pockets for cash to buy food in town. When they finally exhausted their efforts and ideas, all they could produce were five loaves and two little fish donated by a boy in the crowd. This meager meal in Jesus' hands, however, was more than enough.

When Harvey and I gained custody of his daughters, our household swelled from four to seven. This meant a much larger grocery bill, more laundry, less hot water for showers and baths, higher utility bills, a lot more housework, and gallons more gas for running kids to and from school and other activities. Making our dollars and time stretch while maintaining our family in some semblance of order was a real challenge—one we couldn't have met without Jesus stepping in with a miracle.

If I had to use one word to describe our home after the girls came to live with us full time, it would be *chaos!* No one could find clothes to wear, and half the kids went without their baths because we never considered how long it would take for a family of seven to get in and out of the tub or shower—not to mention how long the hot water would last. We had to provide several dollars every day for school lunch money. Forget the sack lunches—we didn't have the time or groceries to pack them. Every morning, bickering and arguing among the siblings rattled the walls and everyone's nerves. We were anything but organized when the kids were finally dropped off for school—late. Something had to give.

Our family was like a house with a bad plumbing job. We had leaks in our pipes where money, time, and effort were wasted in every area. It was as if I was running around with a roll of duct tape, trying to fix all of them. As soon as I would tape up one leak, another would spurt out on the other side of the house. I was worn out, and my roll of duct tape was exhausted.

After reading every book I could find on organizing time and money, I had neat closets, but I still felt just as helpless and empty-handed as the disciples. Some say that necessity is the mother of invention, but I say insanity is the motivator of intercession. Organization began in my prayer closet—not my clothes closet. I asked God to show me how to manage our household. He began by helping me identify the leaks.

FIXING THE LEAKS

When a household expands to include even one additional person, there is increased pressure to stretch time, money, and efforts. Outgo is increased while income remains the same. The workload is multiplied, but time is not. For most busy moms, time is a commodity in short supply. Before we know it, the increased pressure of financial responsibilities, workload, and time demands causes our pipes to burst.

Like water damage caused by an unattended leak, these pressures will get the better of us if we don't identify and fix them. We must face and repair the damaging stress from these added pressures of blending a family, one leak at a time. Our family was no exception. The gavel fell—God was calling our family to order.

Every family has its own little pressures and problems, causing leaks to spring up in their day. By taking these pressures to the Lord and asking for his wisdom, you will surely identify your leaks and find practical solutions. Try objectively to examine your family as if you were an outsider looking in. In other words, remove your own personal emotions from the situation long enough to put each problem in perspective. If lost shoes are a problem in your mornings (as they were in ours), instead of overreacting in anger toward the child and letting the pressure over a small thing build, look to the Lord for wisdom and a practical way to fix the problem early on.

By the time I realized what was happening in my home, I had allowed the pressures to build to the bursting point. The small things—like looking for lost shoes when it was time to leave, or discovering clean folded clothes in the hamper between dirty socks and muddy jeans—were blown out of perspective. Practical, normal responses to these situations gave way to explosive frustration and anger. These "dripping pipes" can easily steal our peace. Many of them, however, can be patched up before they do any serious harm. The trick is in locating the drip before it has time to burst.

Many mothers face the dilemma of running from early in the morning until collapsing into bed at night, especially if they work outside the home. I don't claim to be an expert on time management, but I *am* a woman. Women, by nature, are adaptable to multitask situations. For instance, a woman can easily stir a pot of sauce on the stove, settle a dispute between children, kiss a child's boo-boo and wipe away their tears, answer the phone, say a quick prayer with the caller, and set the table for dinner—all with a baby on her hip. Because we women are multitask pros, and we usually manage the household, it only stands to reason that we would want to make the tasks—and steps to do them—fewer and shorter.

Between packing lunches, finding clothes to wear, brushing hair, and signing papers, I felt like an untrained, out-of-shape marathon runner with a charley horse and shin splints, stumbling onto my knees. After spending a good deal of time praying on my skinned-up knees, God showed me how a marathon runner begins by preparing himself for the race ahead. He doesn't begin his race at the starting line—his race begins in the training and conditioning. He studies his daily runs, find his stress-causing weaknesses, and corrects them. If the runner properly prepares himself, stress on his muscles won't bring him down during the race. I realized I could condition myself for my race too. There were several things that could be consolidated to save time, steps—and stress.

STRESS-BUSTING SOLUTIONS

My first stress buster had to do with baths and clothes. Children's baths and showers were taken at night to eliminate the morning rush for the bathroom. After their baths the kids laid out what they would wear to school the next day. Laying out the clothes included *finding their shoes.* Somehow, shoes seemed to walk away from where they had been left the night before, engaging the kids in a time-consuming game of hide-and-seek. By having school clothes and shoes laid out the night before, we also eliminated those last-minute searches in the morning.

More often than I care to count, we were caught by surprise without clean pants or socks when everyone was getting ready for school. But because of our new system, I was able to wash the needed items of clothing the night before, instead of discovering the "dirty" little surprises the next morning.

Our second stress-busting solution had to do with school-related paperwork—notes from teachers, school papers to be signed, and homework. Schoolwork was taken care of before baths, thereby avoiding staying up late to finish projects and assignments. If homework assignments or notes from teachers went unaddressed, they would most likely forget it—sometimes on purpose. Few things got my dander up faster than those last-minute details as we were rushing out the door, accompanied by "I forgot." By doing this prep work the night before, a lot of stress was eliminated from our morning routine—resulting in fewer leaks when the pressure was on.

Once the "night before" routine was set in motion, I had to determine the morning routine. School mornings were chaotic in those early days. At first, everyone was coming into the kitchen at different times while I packed the lunches. They wanted me to get their breakfast, find their clothes, or fix their hair. Some came into the kitchen as soon as they woke up, while others dawdled, taking their time getting dressed. A couple of the kids decided they didn't want to eat—only to complain on the way to school that they were hungry and could we stop at McDonald's!

Continued prayer brought simple, workable solutions to mind—like setting out bowls, spoons, cereal, and milk on the counter before the kids got up. We told the kids, "No one is allowed in the kitchen until they are fully dressed, complete with socks and shoes." Once they were dressed, they could come to the kitchen and eat. Their breakfast was ready and waiting when they got there. We also reminded them of the long wait for the lunch bell at school if they didn't eat.

Because I didn't have room in the refrigerator for all the lunch boxes to pack them the night before, I packed lunches in the morning while the children ate their breakfast. With all the lunches packed, my hairbrush and I worked our way down the line of little girls eating cereal at the kitchen bar. Brushing through their hair, I asked each one, "How do you want your hair today—French braids, ponytail, or half up and half down?" While they ate, their blonde strands were put in place for the day. Amazingly enough, we even had time for a short family Scripture reading before we went to school. Through prayer and planning on skinned-up knees, peace and order had finally come to our school mornings.

These may seem like obvious things to do, but in an active household, the obvious can easily be overlooked. I'll admit, I did have to give up a little more time on the couch in the evenings, but I rested peacefully at night knowing my leaks were repaired by the Master leak-fixer.

Pinching Pennies 'til They Scream

Our miracles came through prayer. We laid our needs daily before the Lord. God answered our prayers by giving us the necessary wisdom to manage our time and finances. During our early years of blending, money was very tight. Though we owned our own business, there were weeks during our slow seasons when we couldn't draw a paycheck. Naturally, those were the weeks one of the kids needed extra money for a field trip or a pair of shoes because the old ones were pinching their toes.

Around the Clark house, we did a lot of pinching. We pinched our pennies until they screamed. Pinching and screaming reminds me of a story Harvey tells about his mother. Growing up, Harvey and his family attended church regularly. During the long sermons, if he got a little squirmy (as boys often do), his mother would calmly reach over, get a good hold of the fleshy part of his upper arm, and pinch it real hard. He never screamed out loud in church for fear of his life, but she held on until he straightened up in his seat. He learned from experience the consequences of inappropriate actions and behavior in church. His mother's pinching had its desired effect.

I pinched my pennies, much like Harvey's mother pinched his arm. I held on until I got what I wanted from them. Like the disciples, I brought my meager loaves and fishes to Jesus. I prayed, and somehow or another, there was always enough. In fact, many times we had leftover remnants to make use of later.

Leftover remnants can come in the form of food, money, time, or work—anything that can be salvaged by using God's wisdom in organizing and running a household efficiently. Packing lunches is a prime example of how I was able to save time, money, food, and work.

Five sack lunches five days a week took some strategic planning. About twice a month I made a trip to the discount bread store. My buggy was filled with several loaves of day-old bread, which I kept in the freezer. I always took advantage of the low prices, stocking up on a variety of snack cakes and fruit pies. When I got home, all the snack cakes and fruit pies would be dumped into a basket in the pantry. These snacks were off-limits except for lunches.

In the morning, I carried this snack basket from room to room as I woke the kids up for school. They wiped the sleep from their eyes as they picked out a snack for their lunch. I lined up the chosen snacks on the kitchen counter by age of the child so I wouldn't mix them up. Then in front of each snack I would lay out the bread for sandwiches. I knew who liked mayonnaise and who hated mustard, so my assembly line ran pretty smoothly. After I made the sandwiches and laid out the snack and fruit, everything went into their lunch boxes. If there was an uneaten snack cake or piece of fruit from the day before, it went back into the basket or refrigerator. Five lunches were packed five days a week for five kids in five minutes. A teacher once commented that the Clark lunches were the envy of the school cafeteria.

Every family is different. Consider your children's ages, attitudes, and all the things that contribute to pressure in your particular situation. The best way to do this is to examine prayerfully the overall situation and the goal you are trying to accomplish, minus the emotional ties to your children and spouse. While trying to get everyone to church, to school, to do homework, or to do chores, what are your biggest obstacles? In other words, look for the pressure spots and identify the leaks.

After you identify the leaks, sit down with your spouse behind closed doors and communicate. Talk it through until you have a plan of action. Pray together to determine how you will introduce this plan to your family. Take into consideration all the tender spots between stepparent and stepchild, as well as how much you are willing to bend until the children adjust to the plan. If stepparent relationships are still volatile, let the biological parent explain the how-tos and where-fors of your new plan. Keep in mind: your goal is to fix the leaks and reduce the pressure in the household, not add to it.

When Jesus asked the disciples to feed the multitude, his intention was to teach them to look to him. When we are faced with the impossible, Jesus beckons us to put our faith in him as well. When we hand him our meager provision against an insurmountable need, he compassionately takes it and multiplies it, filling our leftover baskets with remnants beyond what we could think or ask. The key is putting it into his hands. As long as we hang on and try to do it ourselves, in our own wisdom and strength, we are going to come up short. Jesus took the bread and fish the disciples handed him and broke them into small bite-sized pieces, filling one basket after another. After that, all the disciples had to do was pass them out to the crowds and gather up the remnants. I don't know how big their baskets were, but even one basket filled with broken pieces of bread and fish is more than they started with.

I imagine the disciples were feeling a little anxiety over the idea of feeding the multitude. We experience the same anxiety when the pressure is on for us to make our time and money stretch beyond its natural boundaries. This is the beauty of faith. The Bible says "faith is the assurance of things hoped for, the conviction of things not seen" (Heb. 11:1). In Jesus' hands, even a handful of fish and bread becomes a feast.

Chapter Fifteen

Long Hours/Short Days: Tips for Saving Steps, Time, and Money

She looks well to the ways of her household,
And does not eat the bread of idleness.
~ Proverbs 31:27

There never seem to be enough hours in the day to get everything done. Keeping up with the laundry and running a taxi service for the kids consumes every minute, so how do you find time for sending out Christmas cards or just having a quiet moment to yourself? Extra chores and incidentals seem to get shoved aside for when we "have a minute." Unfortunately, that minute never comes, and all those little things pile up, becoming a mountain too big to climb.

Meeting oneself coming and going is a common pastime in the blended family, but believe it or not, there are ways to keep the small stuff small. Using our time efficiently takes a little planning and practice, but the end result is less pressure, dollars that last longer, and more time for yourself. In my years of blending and taking care of a big family, I found the old saying "Necessity is the mother of invention" words to live by. Tricks to free up extra dollars and minutes were born out of my need for more of the time and money that always seemed to come in short supply.

This chapter is a compilation of tips and ideas for overcoming the traps that rob us of time, money, steps, and bubble baths. These ideas were developed out of my own trial-and-error experiences, as well as a few tips from others who have blended their families successfully. You are probably doing some of these things already, and I realize that not every suggestion is practical for every family. But you never know—you may discover a few golden nuggets among them that will make your life a little more manageable. You might even find a couple of dollars to buy a few scented candles and some extra time to soak in a nice bubble bath.

TIME OUT! MAKING USE OF DOWNTIME

Think about your "downtimes"—the times you are just sitting and waiting. I found myself waiting in the parking lot for the kids to get out of school, waiting in the doctor's or orthodontist's office, or waiting at the ballpark for practice to finish. A busy mom does a lot of waiting. Time spent waiting doesn't have to be time wasted. In fact, it actually can be quite productive. Try some of my suggestions, and you may just knock out a few of those jobs you never seem to have time for *and* amaze your family and friends with your efficient use of time.

TOTE BAG WISDOM

Something I learned from my best friend was to keep a tote bag in my van all the time. My bag stayed in the van even when I went into the house—that way I wouldn't forget it in my usual rush out the door. The tote bag contained everything from blank thank-you notes, birthday cards, stamps, and my address book to cookbooks, my Bible, and a good novel. Read on and I'll show you why.

Christmas cards: Long before the holiday season began, I had my Christmas cards and list in my bag. By writing out a few cards each day and mailing them once a week, the job was done early enough for the recipients actually to enjoy them *before* they opened gifts on Christmas morning.

Note and birthday cards: Use your waiting time to write a note to a friend or send a thank-you. At the beginning of each month, make a list of family and friends who have birthdays that month. Keep your list and a box of birthday cards in your bag. Your downtime can be used to write a short, thoughtful note in a birthday card, and it will be ready to mail—before their birthday. If you really want to wow them, figure out the date you should send it so the card arrives on their actual birthday. To be sure it is mailed on time, put the mail date (not the actual birthday) in the corner of the envelope where the stamp goes. When the mail date arrives, stick a stamp on the envelope covering the mail date and drop it in a drive-by mailbox. The job is done, and everyone will be impressed that you remembered their birthday!

Bible study and journaling: Keep a small Bible and a devotional book in your bag. Although I wouldn't recommend this as your only devotional time, it can certainly be a spiritual and emotional boost for your otherwise stressful day. Reading a chapter or two from an encouraging book during downtimes also provides a nice way to relieve stress. You may even want to spend some of this quiet time in the car writing in a journal.

Meal plans and shopping lists: Meal planning can be a great use of downtime. If you have wanted to try out a few new recipes, but you haven't had time to browse through your new cookbook, drop it in your car tote and take it with you. I've actually come up with a few family favorites while the kids were at ball practice and piano lessons. Jot down the ingredients you'll need to create your new dish, and guess what? You'll have your list with you in your car tote when you go to the grocery store. (I'm sure none of you have ever done this, but I have a tendency to leave my grocery list on the kitchen counter in my rush to get out the door and to the store.)

TECHNOLOGY TIME SAVERS

Technological advances have made it possible for busy mothers to do many things "on the go" that were not possible before.

Return calls: Take advantage of the awesome technology of cellular phones. Make appointments, return calls, and conduct business in the car while you're waiting for the kids to get out of school, baseball practice, or the movies. Don't try to do this while you are driving, though—your kids and the road need your undivided attention.

Portable office: With laptops and pocket computers, anyone can set up a portable office in their car. I keep all my finances on my computer and can actually balance a checkbook while I'm waiting in a parking lot. You'll be pleasantly surprised how these chores done in the car will free you up in the home.

GIMME A BREAK!
CONSERVING IN-HOME TIME AND MONEY

Wouldn't it be nice to light a few scented candles and enjoy a good soak in the tub in the evenings? Did I hear you say you don't have time for that? What? No candles? I felt the same way when making meals, washing dishes, and doing laundry for five kids—six if you want to count Harvey. I was covered up and busy every night until I fell into bed exhausted. I knew there had to be a better way to get these chores done, spend less money, and still have a few moments for me.

MEAL PLANNING AND PREPARATION

You can save a lot of time and money by planning ahead. If you already know in the morning what you are preparing for dinner at the end of a busy day, you can reduce tension levels considerably. Only one word describes what happens when you realize it's five o'clock in the afternoon and you still don't have a clue what you'll make for dinner—*stress.*

Planning your week's meals ahead of time on a shopping list accomplishes two goals: first, it takes a load off your mind by reducing stress; second, it cuts down on impulse-shopping at the grocery store, thereby reducing overspending. You'll end up feeling better and saving money too!

Below are some planning options to try. Pick and choose the ones that function best for your family.

Monthly meal planning: Once-a-month meal preparation takes a little more time and money up front, but having homemade meals prepared and frozen ahead for your family will save even more time and money in the long run. There are several good cookbooks available for preparing meals ahead. If the thought of preparing a month's worth of cooking is too much for you, try a two-week plan and invite a friend over to do it with you. You'll both have great meals prepared ahead, and you'll enjoy good company in the process.

Food prepping: If preparing meals in advance is impractical for your household, try preparing frequently used ingredients ahead. Many meats and vegetables can be prepared ahead and stored in containers or plastic zippered bags for the upcoming week. Try chopping onions, shredding cheese, washing and peeling carrots, boiling and deboning a chicken, boiling eggs, browning hamburger meat, etc.

I always bought family-sized packages of hamburger meat, chicken, and pork chops to separate and freeze. Family-sized packages are cheaper than the smaller ones. Separating the meat doesn't take a lot of time either. You can even make up hamburger patties and meatloaf mix and then put the rest into one- and two-pound packages, or whatever portions you would need for your family. Taking these extra steps ahead of time cuts your nightly meal preparation time considerably.

Two-for-one meals: When making a casserole or stew for dinner, why not make twice as much and freeze the second pan for a night when you don't have time to cook? The ingredients may be doubled, but the time isn't. Instead of making one pan of lasagna, make two and freeze one. Write the date and description of the dish on masking tape, and you'll have a meal prepared ahead for football night, when everyone has to leave the house early.

Coupons and sale items: Plenty of money can be saved by organizing your grocery shopping according to sales. For regular groceries, check the newspaper for sale items and coupons. Local grocery stores often have special coupons in the news-paper for great deals on meat and other items.

If you live in a small town or an area that doesn't have a big city newspaper carrying a good coupon section, ask a few relatives who live in bigger metropolitan areas to clip and send you the coupons your family is likely to use. I have a friend who did this. Her mother, living in Florida, saved her hundreds of dollars by sending an envelope of coupons every week.

Keep your clipped coupons tucked in an envelope in your purse so they are with you anytime you go to the store. Be careful not to buy items you really don't need or normally wouldn't buy if you didn't have a coupon. Numerous books have been written on coupon shopping, so check your local library or bookstore for all the ins and outs of shopping with coupons.

Bread stores: As I mentioned in a previous chapter, I made a regular trek to the bread store for bread and snack cakes. I was truly amazed by how much money I saved by doing this. Bread freezes, so when you find a good deal, stock up! A big family consumes a lot of bread, and those pennies add up.

Shopping in bulk: Consider planning your grocery budget so that you can make a monthly trip to the wholesale club or utilize a co-op for items your family uses in large quantities. Splitting bulk quantities of staple items such as flour and sugar with a friend or two can save everyone money.

If you like to bake, co-ops are the way to go. Wholesale clubs are great for stocking up on paper items, laundry detergent, and canned and frozen goods. However, compare prices with your local grocery store sale ads, because not every quantity-sold item is a bargain. Local grocery stores often have items on sale that are far cheaper than the wholesale club.

"Fend-for-yourself night": Toward the end of the week, when we had several containers of leftovers in the refrigerator, we had what we called "fend-for-yourself night." That night everyone in the family made their own dinner. They were allowed to pick a leftover from the refrigerator or create their own dish. The only rule was that they had to clean up after themselves. "Fend-for-yourself night" gives mom a break from cooking, and the leftovers won't go to waste.

Taking turns: When mom and dad both work, preparing the end-of-the-day meal can be wearisome. The responsibility of cooking and cleaning up makes the job lighter and less of a burden on mom if her husband and older children take a regular turn in the kitchen. Some children are more apt to do this than others.

Two of our daughters loved the opportunity to create some culinary delight; the other two didn't know, or care to know, one end of a spoon from the other. All of us were better off leaving Aaron out of this whole notion of cooking altogether, but Harvey was a pretty fair chef. He got carried away with the spices from time to time, but it still gave me a break from the job. Every family is different. Saving energy and time is your goal, and if you can accomplish this by taking turns in the kitchen, it is worth a shot.

Cleanup: If your husband and kids are not suited to cooking, they can certainly help in the cleanup. Assigning a cleanup night usually works in most families. If assigning a cleanup night isn't possible, have every family member clear their place at the table when they are finished eating. Even my three-year-old grandson is trained to do this (although you may want to check the trash can for loose utensils after the toddlers leave the kitchen).

LAUNDRY

Laundry can be the most depressing and overwhelming chore in a family. A continually overflowing laundry bin can easily set anyone into a spin cycle. Try some of these laundry tips, and I guarantee you'll save some wear on your wash day.

Individual hampers: I found it much easier to keep up with washing clothes by setting a laundry hamper in each bedroom. This item makes two big jobs smaller. The first is keeping dirty clothes off the floor. A child will more likely take the initiative to put their dirty clothes in the hamper if one is right there in the room.

The second job made smaller involves sorting. When you are ready to wash white clothes, tell everyone to bring their white clothes to you in the laundry room. Do the same for dark colors, towels, and jeans. The kids learn to sort clothes, and they won't be teased about wearing pink athletic socks when they go to school.

Courtesy rule: As our children became teenagers, capable of bearing some of the bigger household chores and responsibilities, they began doing their own laundry. Our number one laundry rule had to do with being courteous. In a big family like ours, someone always had a load in the washer or dryer. When the next person came along to wash their load, they had to abide by the courtesy rule. If they found a load of clothes in the washer or dryer, the person in front of them was asked to finish up their load of washing. If that person wasn't home at the time, the courtesy was for the one doing the next load of laundry to go ahead and put the previous load in the dryer, folding any dried clothes instead of stuffing them in a basket to get wrinkled. The same courtesy was extended to them when the situation was reversed.

Folded clothes: Children as young as age two or three (with a little help of course) can learn to put away folded clothes. This begins teaching them responsibility, and hopefully the lesson will stay with them until they are old enough to move out on their own. When I did the laundry for our big family, there wasn't enough space to keep all the folded clothes in my small laundry room until the kids came and got them. So after folding the clothes, I laid them on everyone's bed. When they came home from school, everyone knew it was their responsibility to put their clothes into their drawers or to hang them up. This chore taught them responsibility for their own clothes, and they knew not to ask mom or dad where their clothes were.

Shelves for clothes: Small children have trouble reaching and opening dresser drawers. That's why my daughter Jennifer has low shelves in her sons' closet for their clothes. Her boys can see and reach the shelves when they need to put their clothes away or find clothes to wear. They also have baskets for socks, underwear, and pajamas. The boys can easily put their folded clothes away, keeping their room tidy and learning responsibility at the same time.

Sock basket: One of my most dreaded and hated laundry chores was the whole sock sorting ordeal. Between the sock-eating washing machine and the mystery of the fifteen hybrid tube socks without mates, it was no small wonder that anyone ever had two matching socks to wear at the same time. My solution was the sock basket. I kept a small basket in the laundry room for stray, mismatched socks. If while folding a load of clothes I couldn't find a mate for a sock, I would check the sock basket. If there wasn't a mate there, I just added the stray to the basket for matching later. Some of those poor, lonely, mismatched socks never did find their mate, but the ones that did were socks I didn't have to replace.

STORAGE

Most of us don't have room for all the things two families blending together accumulate. Harvey and I had stuff crammed everywhere: under the beds, in the closets, and on every shelf. We even rented a storage unit to hold the overflow! My solution was to make the best use of storage space with stackable, see-through plastic boxes. Few frustrations compare to digging through a bunch of cardboard boxes trying to find your Christmas decorations or winter clothes.

Winter Wear: Did I mention that we live in Arkansas? Our winters are pretty mild here, but once or twice during the season we'll get a good snow or have an ice storm. That's when I had to go hunting for all the gloves, hats, scarves, and long johns everyone forgot they had. Every year someone was caught without gloves or a hat, when I knew I bought them for everyone at Christmas.

My solution? Box them up. As soon as the sun melted the snow, I bought an inexpensive see-through plastic box. I then went from room to room and gathered up all the gloves, hats, scarves, thermal underwear, and wooly socks I could find. Everything went into the box and onto a shelf in our storage closet. The next time we had a snow day, out came the box, and everyone was warm.

Toy rotation: Do your small children have so many toys that they get bored with them? This little trick is the secret to making more room in your children's bedrooms *and* taking the boredom out of old toys. When your children are away, box up half of their toys. Make sure you box the ones they seem to have lost interest in—not the ones they play with now. Put the box away where they won't see it.

In about six months, you'll probably notice your children losing interest in the toys you left out for them. When you see this happen, pull the ol' switcheroo trick on them. Bring out the box of old toys and swap them for the others, always leaving the ones they play with all the time. Your kids won't miss the ones they've tired of, and it'll feel like Christmas morning when they see all their old friends back in their room.

Gift box: Birthdays, anniversaries, and baby and bridal showers always seem to catch me off guard. When I need a gift, I either don't have the time to run to the store and buy one, or I don't have the extra money to afford it. The solution is to keep a gift box stocked all year. Whenever you're shopping, watch for sale or clearance items that would make great gifts. If you happen on a close-out sale of baby items, pick up a couple of nice gifts and drop them in your gift box to give away at the next baby shower. Do the same for birthday, anniversary, or bridal gifts. I have found everything from picture frames to baby keepsake boxes on clearance tables. If the gift is already in your gift box, you won't be caught without a gift when that shower invitation or birthday arrives, and you'll have saved money because you bought it on sale.

Wrapping box: Always buy your Christmas wrapping paper after Christmas, when all the stores mark it down to get rid of it. Put it away for the next season. But where do I keep it, you might ask? Discount stores sell plastic boxes specially designed to hold wrapping paper, ribbon, and wrapping accessories. Having a wrapping box stocked with a couple of different papers for birthday, bridal, and baby gifts; scissors; tape; and ribbon will make gift giving easier for you, especially if you can pull the gift out of your gift box. Keep one for Christmas paper and one for the other gift-giving papers. These wrapping boxes fit nicely under a bed and are out of the way when you don't need them.

SHOPPING CENTS

If I were looking for a mentor to teach me how to get the most for my shopping dollar, I would go to my best friend, Cynthia. She is the best bargain hunter I know. She treats every little shopping decision as if it were her last dime being spent. I've accused her of being a tightwad, but she prefers to wear the title "frugal." Cynthia loves nothing more than to rummage through a department store rack during the "½ of ½ of ½ off" sale to find some wonderful little top at a next-to-nothing price.

Recently, my frugal friend set her sites on buying a new -digital camera. This, to Cynthia, was a very big decision. She studied all the different models of cameras in her price range on the Internet and in the catalogs. For months, every time she saw someone take a picture with a digital camera, she asked them a hundred questions. She grilled them on what they liked and didn't like about it. She asked them how much it cost, if they felt they got a good deal, and what kinds of features it had—will it do this, or will it do that? I feel sure the poor, unsuspecting strangers thought they were part of some kind of TV reality game show—*The Photographer's Challenge.*

Cynthia never buys anything without first making sure her need is justified. She then thoroughly studies her purchase to determine if it is exactly what she wants. Finally, she counts the cost to be sure it is worth the money and is within her predetermined price range. If, and only if, all the criteria have been met, she triumphantly makes her purchase. When Cynthia actually brought a camera home, I really thought we should have had some sort of celebration to commemorate the day.

Cynthia's method of assessment is a good approach to shopping for anything from clothes to digital cameras. In this section, I have compiled some of Cynthia's favorite tips, as well as some I've gathered from other girlfriends in the know.

Bargains in the back: When you enter a clothing store, pretend you have blinders on your eyes and walk past all the new arrivals to head straight for the back of the store. That's where they hide the sales and clearance racks. This rule also applies to many home decorating and craft stores. Don't be afraid to ask the sales clerk about any unadvertised sales either, because you won't know if you don't ask.

Boys department: Quoting my frugal friend, "One of the unfair ways of the world is to sell boys' and men's clothes cheaper than girls' and women's." My friend overcomes the world by shopping in the boys' department. White socks and T-shirts are virtually the same for boys and girls, but the boys' are cheaper. She buys her own white socks in the boys' -department because boys' socks are the same size as women's. Try it, you'll like it!

Gift bags: Cynthia says never, never, never buy gift bags anywhere but a dollar store. A dollar store is a Dollar General, Family Dollar, or any other store that advertises the majority of its items at a dollar or at a super discount. Why spend five dollars for a pretty gift bag when you can get it for a dollar? Dollar bags are just as pretty and far more practical for gift giving. The same goes for wrapping tissue and cards.

Holiday and Birthday Helps

Holidays and birthdays bring families together like nothing else. Blended families especially need these times to make us *feel* like a family; but if our holidays become a heavy burden, we can't enjoy them. In our home, I always tried to make holidays and birthdays special; but in doing so, I often wore myself out—not to mention my dwindling bank account. Our homes have enough stress without the added pressures of birthday and holiday preparations. Preparations, however, are necessary. This, my friend, is a classic catch-22.

In my efforts to overcome holiday and birthday stress, I learned to be creative in my preparations and my shopping. Every little step and dollar saved was one less straw on this camel's back. Hopefully, these tips will help you lessen the burden of what would otherwise be a heavy load.

Gifts for Easter baskets or Christmas stockings: With our house full of children, it cost a small fortune to fill Christmas stockings and Easter baskets. Quite by accident, I discovered that the local dollar store had chocolate Easter bunnies, stuffed toys, and candy—all for a dollar. To my surprise, I found I could even get the Easter grass and baskets much cheaper than in a regular discount store. The same goes for stocking stuffers, chocolate Santas, small toys, and candy. Before you go anywhere else, check out the dollar stores. Just make sure you get there early, because holiday treats go fast.

Cookie exchanges: It wouldn't seem like Christmas if we didn't have homemade Christmas cookies for the kids to enjoy. Cookies, however, take a lot of time to bake—and who has time, right? The answer is the cookie exchange. A cookie exchange occurs when several women bake two or three dozen cookies each and then come together to exchange them. You leave with the same amount of cookies you brought, but instead of one kind of cookie, you have several. Depending on how many you want to bring, you can actually have a nice variety of homemade goodies to take home to your family.

Shop early: If I had to buy all the Christmas gifts for my family in the two months before Christmas, it would put us in the poor house every year. My answer is to shop early. All year long I have Christmas on my mind. Whenever I see an item on sale that screams someone's name, I buy it and put it away for Christmas. If it is clothing, I put it in a gift box and write the recipient's name or number (see next tip) on the bottom of the box. If it is something else, I stick a file folder label on the object and write their name or number on it. Keep all your gifts in a locked closet or a secure place to protect your curious "cats" from a certain fate.

Numbered lists: I keep track of the Christmas gifts I have bought with a numbered list. I assign everyone on my list a number. For example, Harvey is 1, Jennifer is 2, Mandi is 3, etc. All the gifts are labeled with a number until it is time to wrap them. I record what I buy on a list and put the person's number by the gift like this: blue shirt-1, picture frame-2, pink sweater-3.

When it comes time to wrap the gifts, I know who each present belongs to by looking at the numbers on the gifts. Gifts aren't duplicated because I have an ongoing list of everything I've purchased throughout the year. I keep this list in my wallet and protect it like gold. One word of caution though: keep your list in a very safe place, because if you lose it, I guarantee you will have one very interesting Christmas morning. How do I know? The year

I lost mine, we literally had a gift exchange when everyone opened each other's gifts.

Hired wrapping: Because my family is so big, wrapping Christmas gifts is one of those dreaded chores I never have time for. One year, our church had a fund-raising drive for the youth group by setting up a stand for wrapping Christmas gifts. I loved it so much, the next year when they didn't have the fund-raiser, I just hired a couple of teenage girls to come to my house and wrap gifts. I set up some card tables and a trash can in the living room with all the wrapping supplies. I served hot cocoa with marshmallows and played Christmas music while they wrapped gifts. The girls earned a little Christmas shopping money, and my chore was done in an afternoon—stress free. It was worth every penny.

Christmas labels: This idea came to me when I hired the teenage girls to do the Christmas wrapping. Because we have such a big family, Christmas tags can get expensive and confusing—especially when the ones wrapping don't know how to spell everyone's name. I have one of those fun greeting-card programs on my computer with a lot of different holiday -graphics for making cards. Instead of making a card with them, I used pages of file folder labels to make peel-and-stick Christmas tags. I found cute Christmas reindeer, Santas, snowmen, and snowflakes to put beside each name typed in a colorful font. By printing one name for each page of file folder labels, you'll have adorable and cheap peel-and-stick Christmas tags for everyone in the family. If you don't use all the tags on a page, just put them in your wrapping box for next year.

THRIVING, NOT STRIVING

I'm not really an organized person by nature, but I've learned from trial and error that a little organization goes a long way when you're juggling time and money in a big family. Our whole family has enjoyed more fun times together going out for pizza and to movies with the money I've saved by being frugal. In fact, I was able to splurge on a few things that I normally wouldn't even consider, like a manicure, a new pair of jeans, or lunch with a friend.

Moms, don't feel guilty for spending a few moments and a few dollars on yourself. You need it—especially in a blended family. How can you expect to tie your family knot together if you are worn out, frayed along the edges, and all tied up in knots yourself? Believe me, our family knots will tie more easily if we can loosen up a little and relax with some quiet time alone.

What would it mean to you to take a thirty-minute walk, a twenty-minute bubble bath, half an hour for a manicure, or a little time to read a few chapters in a good book? For me, it was peace of mind and refreshment. Call me selfish, but after a long day of laundering, chauffeuring, cleaning, cooking, and working through stepfamily squabbles, I was especially thankful for those moments alone.

While stretching time and money was my original intent in implementing these household tips, I discovered, quite by accident, that our whole family benefited from them. We went from a striving family to a thriving family. Now, if you'll excuse me, I think my bubble bath is running over.

Chapter Sixteen

EMPTY NEST?
BLENDING WITH ADULT
CHILDREN

A generation goes and a generation comes,
but the earth remains forever.
~ Ecclesiastes 1:4

Sitting on the floor of my study, I found myself taken aback by the passing of time. Evidence of the fleeting years was lying all around me in the stacks of photo albums. My new bookshelves had been installed, and while moving the photo albums to the other room, one fell open and I was hooked. The next couple of hours were spent looking back. I pondered a picture of Jodie at age seven—that was when she liked pink. Her whole room was done in pink flowers and stripes—the very room in which I now sat reminiscing.

We turned Jodie's old room into my office after she moved into "the big room." The big room was the large bedroom at the end of the house with its own bathroom. As the oldest child vacated the big room, the next in line moved in until it was their turn to venture out on their own. Jodie, the baby of our family, was the last to move out of the house. Just a few weeks ago I put together a new album with pictures of Jodie's wedding. Now, even the big room is empty.

As I thumbed through vacation pictures, birthday parties, graduations, marriages, and grandkids, I couldn't help but wonder where time had gone. Every page was a memory, frozen in time. No one would ever guess, looking at these pictures, that we weren't always a family.

EMPTY NEST

Harvey and I have now joined ranks with all the other parents redecorating their spare bedrooms. We are commonly referred to as "empty nesters," but I have to ask, "What is an empty nest, anyway?" I don't believe there really is such a thing. Harvey and I may have a few empty bedrooms in our house, but every room is still filled with family.

Our phone still rings daily: "Dad, can I borrow your car while mine is in the shop?" "Mom, how do you make lasagna?" "Harvey, when are we going four-wheeling again?" "Terri, will you and Dad be with me at the hospital for the procedure on Tuesday?"

The strings securing our family knot are connected to our hearts—heartstrings. I know because someone is always tugging on them, and I feel my heart responding. When Harvey and I had all the kids at home, struggling to tie all the loose ends of our family into a tidy little knot, we assumed the issues would eventually fray away as the kids grew into adulthood. We've discovered though, that tying a family knot is a lifetime commitment.

Blended family issues don't cease because the kids change addresses; they just take on another dimension. As long as we are a family, situations and issues unique to blended families will continue to surface at weddings, graduations, births, deaths, and any other important family event involving your children.

Take, for instance, a wedding. Think about who will walk your daughter down the aisle. Will it be her father or stepfather? What if the stepfather has been more involved in her life than her biological father? This is an extremely difficult choice for the bride. The decision is made even harder if one of the parents insists on doing things his or her way. The bride doesn't want to hurt anyone's feelings, let alone disobey a parent's wishes, but only one dad can have that honor. I know of a bride whose divorced mother and father walked her down the aisle together because the mother insisted on it. This wasn't what the bride wanted, but in order to keep peace on her wedding day, she agreed. Another bride avoided the problem by asking her grandfather to walk her down the aisle— the only male who had been with her for her entire life.

A young bride has many things to think about as her big day approaches. Seating everyone is another dilemma. Who will sit by whom? Which seats denote more importance? Worrying over where to seat mom and stepmom, dad and stepdad, grandma and stepgrandma puts her under a lot of pressure. A nervous bride doesn't want everyone glaring at one another or fighting during her wedding or the reception. She wants everyone to be there to celebrate and enjoy the day with her. If there is animosity between the child's parents, a wonderful experience could become a disaster.

On Jodie's wedding day, after Harvey walked his beautiful, baby girl down the aisle, and the minister asked, "Who will give this bride?" Harvey wasn't sure how to respond. The standard response, "her mother and I," wouldn't work because the word *mother* could refer to Jodie's mother or to me, Jodie's stepmother. If

Harvey responded, "I do," it would exclude both mothers. Harvey didn't want to offend or exclude anyone, so he ended up saying, "Her family and I." His choice of words was a brilliant answer to a potentially explosive question.

Weddings, as well any other situations bringing both sides of the family together, require a certain measure of restraint and maturity. Our kids aren't asking us to be chummy with our exes—they just want us to be civil. Proverbs 19:11 says, "A man's discretion makes him slow to anger, and it is his glory to overlook a transgression." For our children's sake, we should exercise restraint and overlook remarks and attitudes, no matter how frustrating or uncomfortable we might be. Many events—such as weddings, funerals, births, and graduations—only come once in our children's lives. How sad it is for them to have them ruined by petty jealousies or power struggles between their parents. Remembering our children and the reason we are gathering together in the first place is always a good incentive to hold our tongue.

FIRST FLIGHTS

Harvey and I are enjoying our empty nest, but for some -reason it keeps getting emptier. Our kids keep flying back home to snitch a piece of our nest to build their own. Every time I turn around, something else leaves the house.

This is what happens: one of the kids moves into an apartment and needs a dresser. They come by the house and nonchalantly ask, "Mom, you don't use this old dresser anymore, do you? Can I have it?" Of course, I'm not actually *using* it, so the next thing I know, I'm at the furniture store buying a new dresser to fill the empty space in my spare room. The last time I bought a new set of glasses, the kids descended like vultures on the old ones. And guess where they do their grocery shopping when they are out of food and money? Give up? Mom and dad's house. Harvey and I really don't mind. We love having our family around us, and who needs all the clutter anyway?

Of course, these are just small things. I wouldn't have given up the dresser, glasses, or food if they really mattered to me. However, extending help to our adult kids raises the question of responsibility. After the kids leave home, we do have to set some limits on how much we will help them. After all, we don't want them cleaning us out of house and home.

Consider a college student living away from home on a budget. He has enough money to meet all of his needs every month but depends on his parents to give him more money to go out with friends. He always comes up with a good excuse for running out of money early, but in truth, asking dad for money is easier than cutting back on eating out with friends.

As long as dad is willing to hand money to his adult child, the child will continue to depend on it and expect it. If, however, dad sets a limit and enforces it by telling his son no, the young man either eats at the cafeteria or goes hungry. He might think his dad is being mean, but he'll remember the growl in his stomach the next time his friends invite him out.

A little hardship goes a long way in teaching our children responsibility. They learn resourcefulness through adversity. Freedom and responsibility go hand in hand—making adult decisions means facing adult consequences.

While living at home, Mandi was notorious for leaving on all the lights and her stereo when she left for school or went out with friends. Her stereo must have been too loud because all of my instructions and complaining fell on deaf ears. I showed her our electric bill, but because it didn't come out of her pocket, the wheel on our electric meter continued to spin out of control.

After graduation Mandi and a girlfriend rented a house together while they attended college. The first time Harvey and I went to visit them, I noticed it was dark in the house. Mandi had removed all but one lightbulb from every room. As she escorted us through the house, she switched off the light in the room we were exiting before turning the light on in the room we were entering. Surprised, I asked her why she was doing that. Mandi blinked her pretty blue eyes at me and exclaimed, "You should see my electric bill!"

A Place Called Home

Before I met Harvey, the prayer of my heart was to have a home my kids could always come back to. Growing up in a military family, I have no attachments to any particular home. Every time we moved to a new city, I made new friends and lived in a new house. I used to envy those who lived in the same house their whole life, so I always wanted a "real home" of my own. Because I never developed roots in any one place, I desperately wanted them for my children.

After Harvey and I married, God gave me the desire of my heart. Our home is the nucleus and central gathering place for our family. All of our children feel the same way about our home. They may not live here anymore, but they know they are always welcome.

My prayer was to have a place my children could always come back to—but not permanently. There have been times when our kids have had to move back home while they were going through a transitional period, but it has always been understood that any move back home is temporary. Additionally, living at home requires a measure of responsibility on their part. I am not their bank, maid, or laundry service.

When my oldest son, Jeremy, who is in the military, was stationed to Germany, there was a transition period between the time they moved out of military housing in Colorado and their departure date to Germany. Jeremy, our daughter-in-law, Sheri, and their three children moved back home for a few months. Our empty nest was suddenly filled with chicks!

My grandchildren were seven, five, and two. Sheri is a wonderful mother and daughter-in-law. She cleaned up after the kids, did their laundry, and helped with the cooking. Jeremy and Sheri felt comfortable in our home, and Harvey and I enjoyed having the time with them before they left the country. We've had similar home reunions with Jennifer and Aaron as well.

Coming home temporarily is a situation that often happens when our children are young adults. As long as they don't expect to move back into a childhood mentality of dependency, and they are behaving as responsible adults, a temporary flight home is fine.

Situations occur where we have to set some boundaries. If an adult child is acting irresponsibly, with a pattern of taking advantage of those who help him, we are opening a can of worms to let them move back home. As long as the worms are plentiful, the chicks will continue to feed.

BOUNDARIES

While they live at home, we set boundaries for our children's own good. When they are very young, our boundaries protect them from burning themselves or falling down steps. As our children grow, the boundaries still protect, but they are moved to allow room for choices and responsibility. We restrict television time and make them clean their rooms.

As our children move into adolescence and young adulthood, they are given enough rope to venture out of our comfort zone but not enough rope to hang themselves. For instance, when a teen begins to drive, we restrict who they can be with, where they can go, and how late they can stay out. If the kids violate boundaries, parents enforce consequences, such as the loss of their privileges.

Boundaries change when our children leave home. The new boundaries are designed to teach our children to be responsible adults. They no longer keep the children in; they are designed to keep them at bay. These fences promote the independence and self-sufficiency needed to make it in the adult world while protecting the parents from "mooching" children who use guilt or intimidation as a means to get a free ride. If we haven't set up and enforced boundaries when our children lived at home, we will find it more difficult to do so when they become adults because of their established behavior patterns and responses.

Blended family or not, we must set limits for our adult children. If we don't enforce them, we make it easy for our adult kids to move back into an unhealthy state of dependency on us. Kids who have had limits imposed upon them at an early age make and stick to their own boundaries as they move into adulthood. Harvey and I have helped all six of our kids get out of binds from time to time. We were glad to do it, but we aren't paying their way through life. They all work and pay their own bills as responsible adults. Harvey and I feel this is a direct result of consistently enforcing the boundaries we set for them while they were living at home.

No Boundaries

Blood bonds are very strong. For some parents, who truly love their children, it is very hard to see that they are actually doing more harm than good by not implementing hard consequences for misbehavior.

Gary and Susan are friends of ours who had trouble setting and enforcing boundaries in their blended family. At the time of their marriage eleven years ago, they had four children living with them. The younger two were Susan's, while the older two were Gary's. In addition, Gary had two adult children who lived on their own.

Gary is a very nice man with a sensitive, gentle manner—the very qualities that made Susan fall in love with him. Theirs was a marriage made in heaven.

Their problems began when his ten-year-old son, Bill, the oldest of the four children living at home, was diagnosed with ADHD—attention deficit hyperactivity disorder. Because of this, Gary always gave him a little more slack than the other children.

Gary and Susan had standard house rules, such as no eating in the living room and restrictions on when television could be watched. The other three children obeyed the rules, but Bill ignored them.

Because Susan was Bill's stepmother, she relied on Gary to be the disciplinarian. Gary would respond to disobedience by getting angry with his son, but there all correction ended. Bill felt no consequences for breaking the rules other than Dad getting mad. In the beginning, Susan tried to be understanding of Gary's leniency; but as time passed, Bill's behavior grew continually worse. Often, when Susan would tell her husband about something Bill did, Gary would minimize the seriousness of the offense.

In Bill's teen years, Susan and Gary would find cigarettes hidden in his room. Things missing from Susan's parents' home and small items belonging to the other children would turn up in there also. Consequences for this type of behavior were always minimal. Because Bill never suffered more than a verbal reprimand from his parents' anger, his behavior continued down this path into his adulthood. By the time Bill moved out of the house, he was out of control, going so far as destroying property and abusing the other children. At age nineteen he stole a car and ended up in jail. That was the first time Bill actually suffered the consequences for his actions.

Because of his gentle and compassionate nature, Gary had trouble reinforcing his boundaries with meaningful consequences. He felt a measure of guilt and responsibility for his son's emotional state. Knowing the divorce affected Bill harder than the other children because of his ADHD, it was hard for Gary to do more than yell at his son. He made excuses for Bill's behavior and sometimes even transferred his anger to the other children.

Whenever Bill lost a job and needed help, he would go to his dad, who would give him money and let him move back into the house, overriding Susan's objections. Gary assured Susan that Bill would have to live by the boundaries they set, but as was the case in the past, he ignored the rules. Susan had to hide her purse, and things were stolen from the other children every time Bill lived at home. The situation would continually grow worse until Gary ended up putting his son in a hotel.

Bill used his father's forgiving nature and guilty feelings to manipulate him. This manipulation caused Gary and Susan's marriage to suffer greatly because she could see what Bill was doing to her husband but could not get Gary to act. The sensitive, gentle spirit that drew Susan to Gary was now the very thing that was driving them apart. She resented Gary always putting his son before her and the other children. His unwillingness to enforce the rules with his son affected everyone in the family. When Bill wasn't living at home, Gary would give him money every time he got himself in a mess.

This situation put a strain on Gary and Susan's finances, as well as their relationship. Susan had assumed that once Bill grew up and moved out, there would be peace in their home. She hoped he would be like Gary's other two adult children who grew up and went on with their lives as responsible adults.

Seeing the pattern continue even after Bill moved out was all Susan could take. She didn't have anything left to give toward her marriage. She felt nothing for Gary and was ready to call it quits.

The last time they had to kick Bill out of their home, Gary promised Susan and the other kids at home that Bill would never move in with them again. Susan saw this as a huge step for Gary. He had never made this promise before, and she knew it was only a matter of time before Bill would show up on their doorstep again, looking homeless and pitiful, expecting to guilt his father into letting him move back in.

When that day arrived, Bill told his dad he had enlisted in the military and needed someplace to stay for about a month until he was due to report. Bill was all cleaned up and appeared to be trying hard to better himself.

Remembering his promise to Susan and the kids, Gary told Bill that it would have to be Susan's decision. Gary arranged for Susan to talk to Bill the next day. Bill told Susan about going into the military and needing a temporary home for about a month.

Susan and Bill had a real heart-to-heart conversation that day. Susan said this conversation with Bill was one of the hardest things she ever had to do. She told her stepson how glad she was that he was trying to better himself. Susan spoke honestly with Bill, explaining how she felt about all of the problems they had endured over the years.

Difficult as the words were, she explained to Bill she couldn't trust him and that he would be the first one everyone would look to if anything turned up missing in the house. She didn't *want* to mistrust him, but she knew she would. It was too soon, and everyone's feelings were still pretty raw. She said she would keep an open mind, and if in six months to a year he was still doing well and there was a permanent change in him, she would reconsider. But right now he could not move back in.

As it turned out, Bill had not really been accepted into the military. If he had moved back in, it would have been the same old story. Bill has tried to go around Susan by making his dad feel guilty; however, the attempts have been fewer and less frequent because Gary has kept the boundaries in place.

Gary and Susan's marriage is back on the right track, and Susan has regained the love and respect she once had for her husband— something she thought was gone forever. The boundaries, now firmly in place around their home, provide a wonderful peace they've never experienced before as a family. Though Bill continues to be a concern, *he* is now responsible for the choices he makes.

An Ounce of Prevention

Families like Gary and Susan's are everywhere you look. Adult children, some even in their fifties, take advantage of their parents because the parents allow it. Mom and dad think they are *helping* their children when they bail them out of jail, take on their debts, or allow them to live at home rent free, all the while doing their laundry and cleaning up after them like children. In reality, parents who do this are actually hindering their children from becoming adults.

When this type of unhealthy dependency takes place in a blended family, the stakes are even higher. In addition to dealing with your children, you are trying to establish your new marriage. Dealing with a spouse's adult children can be like walking a high wire of emotional balance. Children, younger than the ultradependent ones, watch how you deal with broken boundaries—possibly expecting the same exceptions be made for them.

I talked with Susan about how she and Gary managed to hold their marriage together through all the years of their blending with a problem child. Susan told me it took years of professional counseling, prayer, and a solid commitment to their marriage. They also took weekends for themselves at every opportunity. These bed-and-breakfast weekends helped Gary and Susan bring their situation back into focus. When all hope seemed lost and they were depleted emotionally, financially, and spiritually, God held them together.

None of us are perfect parents, and we all love our children. However, as my mom used to say, "An ounce of prevention is worth a pound of cure." If we begin setting and enforcing boundaries for our children while they are young, when they are older, they will keep them on their own without our help.

CUTTING STRINGS

Setting and maintaining boundaries is a good thing for both the parent and the adult child. But what of the responsible child in college who wants to remain connected but suddenly finds the heartstring cut after their parent remarries? Heartstrings are a lifelong connection between parents and their children, regardless of age or distance. Even adult children need that bond.

Even now as an adult with my own children and grand-children, I remain connected to my dad, who lives across the country in California. We don't talk every day, and I don't ask him for money, but the strings are securely attached to our hearts on both ends. He is interested in my life, and I am interested in his.

So, what if the parent remarries after their adult child goes off to college? Is the adult child still a part of the "family"? They should be, but too often parents say, "I've done my job. Sally is a good kid, and she can take care of herself. It's my turn to enjoy my own life." Out come the scissors, and snip, snip, snip go the heartstrings—Sally is on her own. What could have been a lifelong connection becomes a detached relationship.

JENNA'S STORY

Jenna's parents were divorced when she was about eight years old. Jenna's only memories of her parents' life together was yelling and fighting. Her dad dropped out of her life after the divorce, and Jenna lived with her mom, Lisa. Their heartstrings were tied very closely together. The two of them talked about everything and were inseparable.

Brent came into the picture when Jenna was about eleven years old. Brent was a wonderful Christian man with whom Lisa fell in love. Within a year they were married, and things were completely different around the house. Laughter filled all the empty spaces in their home, they all went to church together, and Jenna felt she had a *real* family. Brent was a wonderful stepfather to Jenna, and she adored him.

A few years after the marriage, Brent began to have some serious health problems. Jenna had graduated from high school and was beginning to make plans for college when Brent took a turn for the worse. He died soon after graduation, when Jenna was just seventeen. Brent's death devastated both Lisa and Jenna; those six years together as a family had meant everything to Jenna.

After Brent's passing, Jenna and Lisa drew even closer as mother and daughter. Lisa encouraged Jenna to go ahead with her plans to go to school, so she did. Not wanting to be too far away from her mother, Jenna chose a school nearby.

During Jenna's first year of college, her mother met another man. Ben swept Lisa off her feet, and they were soon married. At first, Lisa and Ben lived in the same town where Jenna grew up, but while she was away at school, Ben's job required that they move to another state.

Being so far from her mother was difficult for Jenna, but she understood the reasons for the move. Lisa and Ben asked Jenna to move with them, but Jenna loved her school and didn't want to change. Jenna's decision to stay in school in her home state turned the tide in her relationship with her mother.

All of a sudden Jenna was on her own. The strings were abruptly cut, and all support, both emotional and financial, ended. The strings weren't cut out of anger or any disagreement. Because she was grown up now, Jenna was just "out of sight and out of mind."

Jenna worked a few jobs to try to keep herself in college, but she soon dropped out. Her relationship with her mother was strained, at best, not because of the money but because she lost the connection she had always had with her. Instead of talking with Jenna and helping her to sort through different options as she had done in the past, Lisa gave her only one choice—moving. The demand for Jenna to leave her school, all her friends, and everything familiar was more than she could do.

Sadly, Jenna's story isn't all that unusual. Mothers who remarry after their children leave for school often find themselves having to choose between her new spouse and her child. The new spouse usually feels no obligation to pay for the adult child's education; and because they have no heartstring attachment, the child is left to fend for himself.

Boundaries are helpful, but they are not meant to be a wall of separation. Jenna's loss was deeper than a college education; she felt abandoned by the one person who had always been there for her. Jenna lost her father in divorce, her stepfather in death, and now her mother in remarriage. Though Jenna is technically an adult at twenty-one, she is still Lisa's daughter. Up to this point, Lisa and Jenna had always enjoyed a very good relationship, but by cutting off the communication link between her and her daughter, Lisa cut the heartstrings that could have been a lifelong connection.

GENERATION TO GENERATION

Boundaries, communication, and a sensitive, discerning spirit are key ingredients for making the glue that keeps our heartstrings securely attached to our adult children. None of us are perfect—we all make plenty of mistakes in our child-rearing years, but both adults and children alike will grow past their mistakes in time.

Likewise, God's Word doesn't say our children will be perfect angels while we are teaching them right from wrong. But it does give us hope and a promise that our training will have its results eventually.

Time truly does fly by faster than a speeding bullet. Blink an eye and our kids are having kids of their own. Ecclesiastes 1:4 says, "A generation goes and a generation comes, but the earth remains forever." All of this talk of generations coming and going makes me wonder—when did Sara change from tomboy to young women? Is Jodie really a new mommy? How did Jeremy manage to have a family with three children without my noticing? Is Jennifer really a career woman, and Mandi graduating from college? Even Aaron slipped by and found a lovely bride.

Looking through my albums, I saw myself moving along with all the events, but in my heart, time was standing still. Where did the time go? I closed our treasured albums and put them on the shelf, thankful for the time God has given us to watch our children change and grow.

Chapter Seventeen

Mourning Glories: Blending after Widowhood

You have turned for me my mourning into dancing.
~ Psalm 30:11

It seemed as if the entire community was grieving with her. Rhonda was just thirty-two years old when her husband, Marty, had been diagnosed with cancer. Six short, but tortuous months later, he took his last breath. Marty's funeral was the most heartrending service Harvey and I have ever attended. I know God has a special place in his heart for widows. His Word says he will be a husband to the widow and a Father to the fatherless. However, seeing the tears flow from Rhonda and those five children without their daddy just tore my heart out.

They had been a beautiful young family—very active in our church body. At the time of Marty's death, the two oldest daughters, Abby and Haley, were twelve and nine. Daniel was six,

Becky, three, and the baby, Lance, was just eighteen months. Marty and Rhonda lived their lives with absolute faith and conviction. Their dedication to the Lord was evident in their five children. Even Becky, the three-year-old, could quote Scriptures better than some adults.

Marty's death took us all by surprise. Our church family did what we could to help this young widow and her children. We nurtured and prayed for them through every phase of their grieving. Rhonda became everyone's little sister, and her children became our nieces and nephews.

Over the next year and a half, Rhonda made herself rise every morning to do the things she had to do for her young family, but coping with her and her children's grief was almost more than this young widow could handle. Her hopes, dreams, and visions for their family died with Marty. In her mind, she kept rewinding the tape and replaying all the memories.

In a recent conversation I had with Rhonda, she told me that if it weren't for God's mercy and grace, she wouldn't have made it. Rhonda knew God saw each and every tear that fell, but she continually had to remind herself of God's promises to be with her and take care of her.

Rhonda told me that she was finally able to accept God's sovereignty in the timing of Marty's death when he led her to Hebrews 9:27. The Scripture reads, "It is appointed unto men once to die" (KJV). She didn't like the timing, nor did she understand why it had to be so, but she trusted God. Rhonda was confident that God knew her every thought, and he was attentive to her cries for help. He had been faithful to meet her every need materially, emotionally, and spiritually. She finally laid her love for Marty and his untimely death at her Savior's feet.

About eighteen months after Marty's death, Rhonda began talking with a man named Danny. Rhonda and Marty both knew Danny from church, but they had never been close friends. All of us who knew and loved Rhonda had taken on the protective "big brother" role over her and her children. Not just a few eyebrows were raised when it became evident that Danny had an interest in Rhonda, and the interest appeared to be mutual. Of course, "big brother" scrutinized Danny's intentions, but this young man had a reputation as an honest, hard-working man of high moral integrity—he got a thumbs-up from all of Rhonda's big brothers and sisters.

Over the next six months, Danny and Rhonda's friendship blossomed into love. The day they tied the knot, it was standing room only at Trinity Church. The joy and celebration were so exuberant, our church could barely contain them. Rhonda was every bit the radiant bride. Tissue boxes and tears were flowing freely throughout the entire congregation as Danny, Rhonda, and the five children were introduced as a family. God had truly turned their mourning into dancing that day. Tomorrow, however, would be another day.

MORNING GLORIES

Several years ago I lived in a house that had a wall of morning glories climbing up the side of a detached garage. I loved being greeted each morning with the song of brilliant blue blossoms. True to their name, they sang and danced up the wall, filling the air with morning glory. However, as the sun rose higher in the sky, its warmth became too hot for the blossoms to bear. The happy, blue faces disappeared, hiding themselves away until the next morning when they could sing again.

Morning glories come to mind when I think of Rhonda and Danny's early days of marriage. They were so in love, and it was refreshing to see Rhonda and the children smile and laugh again. Like the brilliant blue flowers dancing in the new morning's light, Rhonda, Danny, and the kids seemed happy as a new family.

Blending a family out of widowhood is different from blending a family out of divorce. Yes, children in both circumstances experience pain and loss, but the children who have lost a parent to death have no hope of being reunited with their dad or mom until they get to heaven—a concept difficult for a child to grasp. The new spouse not only has to fulfill the role of husband or wife but also work through the children's grief and rejection. Danny jumped right in to be a husband to Rhonda and a dad for the children, but as the fresh new morning became hot in the afternoon sun, the glory began to fade away.

Afternoon Sun

While the two youngest children, Becky and Lance, were young enough to adjust to the change in their home, the three older children, who had been very close to their dad, began to resent Danny's presence in their lives. Rhonda's oldest daughter, Abby, was very angry with her mother and wanted nothing to do with Danny. Abby's constant state of resentment had its root in her father's last days. She found it impossible to forgive her mother for not allowing her to see her dad before he died. Marty, however, did not want his children to see and remember him in the final stages of his death. Rhonda, honoring her dying husband's wishes, kept the children away.

Before Marty's death, Haley had been a fun-loving, happy little girl with a heart to please. After her father's death, she became angry with God. Haley's grief was manifested in her bad behavior and attitude, which grew increasingly worse. She responded hatefully to both Rhonda and Danny, disregarding all rules and authority.

Daniel's response to his father's death was similar to Haley's, but he rejected everyone else around him—even his schoolmates. Daniel's behavior began to change when Danny stepped in as the new man of the house. While having Danny as the head of the house was a welcome relief for Rhonda, it didn't sit well with the three older children, especially Daniel. After his father's death, and even during his illness, six-year-old Daniel had assumed the "man of the house" role. His mother's marriage to Danny pushed him out of this role. Daniel's anger would not permit anyone to get near him or even touch him.

Each of the three children responded individually to Danny out of their grief and loss, but their common response to Danny's discipline and authority was, "You're not our dad, and you never will be."

Danny tried to be understanding toward the children, assuring them that he knew he was not their real dad. He tried to explain to each of the children that God had placed him there to help their mother raise them. Danny was doing the best he could, but the children rejected every effort he made. The heat of the afternoon sun was bearing down on this new family, and the smiles were disappearing from everyone's faces.

HIDDEN BEAUTY

Thinking again of my garden of morning glories, I had to remember they weren't always beautiful. In the heat of the afternoon sun, my wall of morning glories actually looked dead on their vines; but I knew those little beauties would sing again—when the time was right.

During the day and even into the night, my morning glories kept their beauty hidden away in their tightly coiled blossoms. However, with the promise of the morning song, I knew they were worth the effort to water the vine and pull out any weeds creeping up around their roots.

Children who have lost a parent are like those coiled-up blossoms, refusing to bloom. The blazing reality of death and its pain are difficult to face. Though our children may appear to be lost to us, as long as they are connected to a healthy, watered vine, free of choking weeds, they will bloom again.

Danny and Rhonda somehow had to overcome and pull out the weeds of anger and resentment growing around their children's roots. In the meantime, this young couple had to nurture and water their vines, even when they rebelled and refused to bloom. Danny and Rhonda continued to pull weeds as fast and hard as they cropped up around the children, but both were wearing down. Pulling weeds is hard work, especially when the sun is hot on your back. However, Danny and Rhonda persevered because they could visualize their garden of mourning glories singing again.

Gentle Answers

One day, after a particularly difficult battle with Daniel's anger, Rhonda turned to God and cried out, "Lord, what should I do?" His answer was very clear but seemed almost too simple to have any real effect. In her heart, Rhonda heard the quiet, familiar voice of God saying, "A gentle answer turns away wrath, but a harsh word stirs up anger" (Prov. 15:1). Rhonda immediately recognized that she had been reacting to her children's anger with harsh words. For instance, when Haley spouted off about something Danny may have said or done, Rhonda's reaction would be, "We don't talk like that, young lady!" If Daniel tested the limits, she would scold, "You know better than that!" God showed Rhonda that she was reacting harshly to her children's wrath, and this was only stirring up more anger.

An opportunity to test God's answer wasn't long in coming. One afternoon Daniel, in his anger, misbehaved and talked back to his mother. Instead of reacting as she had in the past with swift, harsh words followed by punishment, Rhonda took the child aside and asked him to explain to her why he was so upset. Realizing he had his mother's full attention, Daniel softened the tone of his complaint. Rhonda listened and gently talked him through it, never raising her voice—even if Daniel did. Instead of pointing her finger and scolding, "You know better than that," she asked him questions that made him think about what was right and what was wrong. Her conversation with her son then concluded in prayer. No longer angry, Daniel walked away satisfied that his mother "heard" him. As the tone in Rhonda and Danny's home began to change, so did the children's attitude.

Recently, Rhonda told me she had been sick in bed all day and night with a virus. Daniel, now eleven, had been on duty to take care of his mom and see to her needs. He hated being stuck inside all day taking care of his mom. He had a bad attitude because he wanted to go outside and play with his friends.

Seeing Daniel's anger beginning to surface, Rhonda asked him if he would pray for her. Daniel prayed a very precious prayer for his mother. Impressed with his prayer, Rhonda asked her son about his relationship with God, and a wonderful conversation followed. Daniel and his mother shared a very special moment together in which Daniel told his mom, "You really bless me, Mom. You've done a good job raising me." Daniel confessed to his mother that he really didn't want to take care of her, but now he was glad he did.

Another big change that occurred in Rhonda and Danny's home was the addition of little Benjamin, God's gift to this precious family. Like baby's breath in a bouquet of roses, his birth brought smiles and joy into the house. Little Benjamin tied everyone together as a family because he belonged to everyone.

LOOKING BACK

I talked recently with a couple who have been married nearly three decades. Both J.D. and Pam were widowed before they married in 1976. J.D. had three daughters, while Pam had a daughter and a son. Everyone in this union had the same thing in common—the death of someone they loved.

Curious to see how the oldest children look back on their years growing up in a blended family out of widowhood, I asked them to share a few of their memories.

Sarah, J.D.'s oldest daughter, who was twelve at the time of his marriage to Pam, told me she had been very close to her mother. Now grown with a family of her own, I asked her what the hardest adjustment was to becoming a blended family. She said it was missing her mom. Sarah remembered her mother being a Betty-Crocker-type mom. She was very domestic—always sewing their clothes and cooking up something good in the kitchen. When her dad married Pam, Sarah thought her stepmother would be like her mom. Pam, however, was a working mom.

Pam was a nurse who had a completely different person-ality from Sarah's mother. Cooking wasn't her "thing," and she didn't sew at all. Sarah said Pam was a wonderful mother, but there was a period of time as a young girl when she wished Pam was more like her own mother.

The differences between her mother and stepmother brought the reality of her mother's death back to the forefront of her mind. Those years of adjustment just made Sarah more keenly aware of her mom's absence. Sarah was quick to point out, however, that she had grown to love and appreciate Pam for who she was. Looking back, Sarah said she wouldn't change a thing about Pam.

Pam helped her stepdaughter overcome these comparisons by *not* competing with Sarah's mother. She didn't try to cook and sew like Sarah's mom; she reached out to Sarah by taking her shopping and doing other things with her. J.D., too, didn't lose his daughter in the blending process. He asked her to help him do his Christmas shopping, just as they did before he married Pam. This small gesture demonstrated to Sarah that she was still her father's helper, as she had been in the first few years after her mom died.

Transitions don't come as easily for children as they do for adults. Children, like Sarah, hold the memory of their deceased parent very close to their heart.

Allison, Pam's oldest daughter, described her father as being a very outgoing and flamboyant risk-taker. He drove a little sports car and liked to fly by the seat of his pants. Her step-father, J.D., was just the opposite. J.D. was more laid back and reserved in his personality.

Though Allison didn't have trouble accepting J.D., she did have to adjust to some major changes in the home. For instance, before her mother married J.D., Allison had been unfamiliar with church. She didn't understand religion; but after the marriage, church became a weekly routine.

Over the years, J.D. and Pam made every effort to treat their five children as "our kids." No separation or distinction was ever made between the children after they stepped into their marriage covenant. However, Pam did jokingly tell me that during a particularly heated argument in the early part of their marriage, one of them said, "Whoever files for a divorce has to take *all* the kids!" I guess neither one was willing to take on that challenge alone, since they have remained married nearly thirty years now.

Growing Shoe Sizes

A stepparent will always come up wearing a smaller size shoe than a deceased parent. Deceased parents become more perfect and flawless as their memories become bronzed by grief. Stepparents, who must administer discipline and daily routines, will never be able to match that standard of perfection in their stepchild's eyes. But if a parent realizes this is happening with the child, they can make the transition easier for everyone.

Rhonda and Danny's biggest obstacle in blending their family seemed to be in filling Marty's shoes. In the children's eyes, the shoes had actually grown several sizes. The three older children couldn't remember how very strict their father had been; they only remembered that he loved them. In his death, Marty had become even bigger than life to the children.

In the beginning, Danny jumped into the role of stepfather and disciplinarian with both feet, wanting to help his new wife out with the children. The children met his attempts to correct them with resentment, anger, and complaints to their mother that Danny was "mean and overbearing." In actuality, Marty had been a much stricter disciplinarian than Danny.

The children responded to Danny's authority and position as a stepfather much like my morning glories responded to the afternoon sun. They closed up tighter than a drum. Danny tried, but he couldn't force the blooms to open. Rhonda found herself always playing the role of mediator between her husband and her children. When it became apparent that the children weren't responding to Danny's authority, he took a step back and let Rhonda deal directly with the children. The young -couple talked through their problems concerning the children until they could come up with a suitable solution. Then, after praying together, Rhonda dealt with the children.

TURNING THE PAGE

Childhood seems to fly by us so fast that we scarcely remember anything really significant, but Allison shared something with me that has stayed with her all these years. Allison recounted how her parents asked her if she wanted to be adopted by J.D. and take his name. She said no, explaining that it would erase her father's memory, and that was all she had of him to cling to. There were never any condemnations or hurt feelings over her choice, and the subject was never mentioned again. But by offering his name to Allison in adoption, J.D. expressed his total love and acceptance of her. Allowing Allison to make this choice and then respecting it confirmed and sealed J.D.'s love in her heart.

A child's security is wrapped up in their parents' presence. Often, losing a parent to death shakes the very foundation of a child's world, causing them to hang on to the surviving parent more tightly. Mom or dad represents the only attachment they have to their deceased parent, so when they remarry, they view the new stepparent as another threat to their security. Not only does a child feel that they're losing their remaining parent to an outsider, they also feel as if they are losing their deceased parent all over again. For this reason, it is crucial that parents reinforce their love for their child.

Rhonda and Danny began looking for ways to praise and show affection. Danny encouraged the older children, especially the girls, to let him or their mother know when they needed special time alone with their mom. He explained to the girls that in such a big family, this need could be overlooked. He assured them that because they were important to him, he would do whatever was necessary to make it happen. However, they would either have to let Mom or him know of their need.

Time and consistency permitted Danny to show the children by his actions that he was there to stay. Whether helping with homework or just being someone to talk to, Danny has demonstrated to the children that he loves them.

Rhonda and Danny are tying their family knot by showing affection, praising their children when they do things right, and by being patient and understanding when they do things wrong. Both parents understand that the children are working through grief as well as blending together as a family. Danny and Rhonda have chosen to talk through their struggles with the children and, when necessary, administer discipline with gentleness and consistency. As a result, Danny and Rhonda are now enjoying a garden full of brilliantly blooming morning glories.

I asked J.D. and Pam if they kept pictures of their former spouses out around their house. Both seemed surprised that I would ask. They said, "Of course we do. To take them down would be to erase an important part of our lives."

Rhonda too, expressed a sincere appreciation for Danny's sensitivity toward Marty's memory. Danny is secure enough in his relationship with his wife that he isn't threatened by Marty. Pictures of him still hang on the walls, and the children talk openly of their dad, recounting all the good times they had together as a family.

In widowhood, fond memories and love will always remain for the former spouse and parent. Over time, grieving decreases in its intensity, but it doesn't go away. Children need time to reminisce and remember deceased parents because they are part of who the children are.

To put away all the pictures would be to pretend Marty was no longer a part of the family. In truth, Marty's memory is very important to the children and to Rhonda. This is not to say that Danny is less important. I liken Marty's memory to reading a book, moving from one chapter to the next. Each chapter builds upon the last until the whole story is told. To remove a chapter would be to leave a hole in the novel. Marty was chapter 1; Danny, chapter 2; and the pages are still turning.

Until Death Do Us Part

We say the words in our vows, "Until death do us part," but we never really think about death separating us. Death is something that happens to someone else, but in truth, death comes to every man and every woman. Our lives are in God's hands.

Rebuilding our lives after such a loss is a delicate matter in which we must look to God for help. God's healing does come to those who call to him. He will wipe away their tears (see Isa. 25:8).

God's Word is full of encouragement for the widows and the fatherless. A widow or widower anchored to the foundational rock of Jesus Christ will stand through the grief and loss of their spouse. God does promise to turn our mourning into dancing and replace the ashes of our grief with a garment of praise (see Ps. 30:11; Isa. 61:3).

Like a refreshing drink of cool water on a hot day, one of the many rewards and blessings of remaining anchored to Christ is finding a new love with whom we can begin to live again. However, couples who are blending a family after widowhood face challenges. Unlike the divorcee who has come out of a broken relationship, a widow or widower and their children have experienced the loss of their loved one by death. Blending after widowhood offers an added challenge to tying the family knot—grief.

Rhonda and Danny, like J.D. and Pam before them, are meeting the added challenges brought on by grief while working through the other issues common to blended families. The night for many couples in this situation may seem long and cold. But God's promise in Psalm 30:5 shows us that this, too, will pass: "Weeping may endure for a night, but joy cometh in the morning" (KJV). Like my little blue flowers, trumpeting the dawn, your family can open and sing once again because God's mercies are truly new every morning.

Conclusion

Looking Forward, Not Behind

Therefore, since we have so great
a cloud of witnesses surrounding us,
let us also lay aside every encumbrance
and the sin which so easily entangles us,
and let us run with endurance the race
that is set before us, fixing our eyes on Jesus.
~ Hebrews 12:1–2

Do you mind if I talk about cars for just a few minutes? I am, after all, married to a full-fledged gearhead. There are those who believe Harvey has motor oil running through his veins. He loves cars and racing. In fact, when we were married, Harvey was a professional race car driver with the Sports Car Club of America (SCCA). Exactly two weeks after we were married, Harvey was racing in Addison, Texas, at an SCCA Grand Prix race. It was a mini-truck series, and his was the only Chevy. I was watching the race from the stands, holding my breath at every turn. All of a sudden, as Harvey cut into a turn, his truck lifted and turned a pirouette on its nose. My heart stopped beating when the truck spun around and landed on its side. I jumped to my feet with a lump in my throat for what seemed like an eternity, waiting for my new husband to emerge.

Finally, from the window of the truck, Harvey pops out, wildly signaling the corner workers. They came running over to him—I thought they were checking to see if he was all right—but no, Harvey wanted help pushing his truck back up on its wheels so he could get back in the race! In a few seconds, my beloved was jumping back in the truck and taking off again! I couldn't believe it. And neither could anyone else in the crowd, cheering him on. I knew then how Harvey got his nickname: "Mr. Tenacity."

Harvey sped around the course for several more turns until the wind caught the hood of his truck. The hood flew up, smashing into his windshield. ESPN showed video clips of him blindly racing off course with his hood plastered to the windshield—Harvey's only claim to fame in TV racing. He tried to jump out of his truck to put it back down to fix the problem, but it was too late. The cracked windshield disqualified his truck, putting Harvey out of the race.

Earlier, when Harvey did his little pirouette performance, the small metal pins holding down the hood had fallen out. Those pins, although only two inches long, were a vital part of the truck. Sadly, a quick technical check could have prevented Harvey from dropping out of the race.

Sometimes Harvey's racing makes a good illustration of life. We are running along just fine in our marriage until we find ourselves spinning out of control and flat on our back. Divorce or widowhood does that to us. In both, we face the death of our marriage—something we always expected to last for a lifetime.

Like Mr. Tenacity, we, too, brushed ourselves off and then jumped right back into the race with a new soul mate and a new beginning.

Getting remarried and starting over was an answer to prayer for both Harvey and me. It probably was for you too. Harvey was everything I wanted in a husband, and more. I knew he would make me happy, and I had every intention of doing the same for him. It didn't matter that we both had kids. When we said our vows, facing the emotionally charged issues of blending a family was the furthest thing from our minds. We felt as though we could work through anything as long as we were together. Most couples entering a second marriage feel this way.

But without Christ as the foundation of our homes, we have only our own wisdom and strength from which to draw. The experiences of our past taint our wisdom, and the weight of our present circumstances diminishes our strength. When we are challenged by power struggles and difficult personalities, we immediately put up our walls.

With Christ as the Rock of our lives, we can overcome any obstacle by relying on his perfect wisdom and limitless strength to see us through. Jesus said he came to give us new life, not just a life with a new mate, but an abundantly rich life—a solid foundation on which to build our lives. In the third chapter of John, when a man approached Jesus to ask him what he was all about, Jesus told the man he must be born again. The man couldn't understand what Jesus meant. After all, how can you erase a lifetime to begin again from your mother's womb? Those past experiences have made us who we are. But Jesus told him that a man must be born again to see the kingdom of God. Jesus came to give us life—real life. Not just a flesh and blood life to breathe air, eat food, have a good time, and die, but a life that has a purpose and direction. He came to give us a more abundant life that doesn't end when we take our last breath.

When we are born into this world, we are born in sin. The Bible tells us that none of us can approach God because he is holy and cannot look upon sin. We can't earn our way to him by living a good life and keeping our noses clean. We all fall short. But God loved us too much to leave us separated from him and without hope. That's why he sent his only Son, Jesus, to pay the only acceptable penalty for sin—death.

Born of a virgin, Jesus was every bit a man while maintaining the deity and holiness of God. After living for thirty-three years, tempted as any other man yet never sinning, he willingly laid down his life on the cross as the holy and acceptable sacrifice for the sins of all mankind. But Jesus didn't just die as any other man. He rose from the dead three days after he gave up his last breath on the cross. After showing himself to hundreds of people over the next forty days, Jesus ascended into heaven, where he alone holds the keys to eternal life. In Revelation 1:17–18, Jesus says, "I am the first and the last, and the living One; and I was dead, and behold, I am alive forevermore, and I have the keys of death and of Hades."

Jesus offers us the keys to eternal life. All we have to do is believe in him, accepting his sacrifice for our sins. When we do this, we are "born again" into God's kingdom. He gives us direction for our lives through his Word, the Bible, and the -ability to overcome any circumstance we find ourselves walking through. As we turn our lives over to God, we immediately begin to see changes in our lives and families.

Putting your trust in Jesus may seem like a small, insignificant thing to do, but like the small, seemingly insignificant pins missing from Harvey's truck, without Jesus we are disqualified from the race. Jesus said in John 14:6, "I am the way, and the truth, and the life; no one comes to the Father but through Me."

Tying our family together into an enduring knot has been one of my and Harvey's greatest challenges. The emotional conflicts we faced over the years severely tested us and our marriage. However, I firmly believe that being anchored to the foundational Rock of Jesus Christ held our family and marriage intact. I could not imagine our marriage surviving without God. We have not only survived the storms and pressures of blending a family, but we are more in love today than when we first said our vows.

Because Harvey is such a car enthusiast, and we have been running with endurance the race together, I have adopted the following passage of Scripture from Hebrews 12:1–2 as my own Scripture to live by:

> Let us also lay aside every encumbrance and the sin which so easily entangles us, and let us run with endurance the race that is set before us, fixing our eyes on Jesus, the author and perfecter of faith, who for the joy set before Him endured the cross, despising the shame, and has sat down at the right hand of the throne of God.

If you are trying to run this race in your own strength, I urge you to do a simple "technical check." Anchor yourself to the foundational Rock of Jesus Christ by accepting his salvation for your sins and placing him in control of your life. You can easily do this right now by praying the following prayer, not just for the sake of your marriage but for your eternal salvation. This may seem like a small technicality, but in the end, you'll find yourself crossing the finish line, having run the race in victory.

DEAR FATHER,

I acknowledge that I am a person lost in sin. I understand and believe that Jesus paid the only acceptable price for my sins on the cross. He obtained victory over sin and death for me when he was resurrected three days after his death. I ask that you forgive me and accept me as a newborn child in your kingdom, to live forever. I ask this in the precious name of your only son, Jesus Christ. Amen.

Endnotes

Chapter One

1. U. S. Census Bureau, 1998.

2. James H. Brady and John Kelly, *StepFamilies: Love, Marriage, and Parenting in the First Decade* (New York: Broadway Books, 1998), 3.

3. George Barna, "Christians Are More Likely to Experience Divorce Than Are Non-Christians," *The Barna Report* (October–December 1999), 9–10.

Chapter Three

1. Rosanne Cash, "A Tribute to June," *Nightflying—The Entertainment Guide* (Harvest 2003), 13, (www.nightflying.com).

2. Ibid.

3. Ibid.

Chapter Five

1. Dr. Seuss Enterprises, L.P., *Green Eggs and Ham* (New York: Random House, 1960).

Chapter Eight

1. Kevin Lehman, *Living in a Step-Family Without Getting Stepped On* (Nashville, Tenn.: Thomas Nelson, 1994), 23.

Chapter Thirteen

1. Larry Burkett with Joseph Slife, "Belief and Behavior," *Money Matters*, Issue: 292 (May 2002).

2. Ibid.

3. This budget plan is from Crown Financial Ministries. Anyone can go to www.crown.org/tools/budgetguide.asp and calculate their budget from Larry Burkett's Online Budget Guide.